# INSIDE THE GRASS HUT

T0115591

三十五世石頭希遷禪師

# INSIDE THE GRASS HUT

## LIVING SHITOU'S CLASSIC ZEN POEM

### Ben Connelly

Foreword by Taigen Dan Leighton

WISDOM PUBLICATIONS · BOSTON

Wisdom Publications
199 Elm Street
Somerville, MA 02144 USA
www.wisdompubs.org

*Library of Congress Cataloging-in-Publication Data*
Connelly, Ben, author.
  Inside the grass hut: living Shitou's classic Zen poem / Ben Connelly; foreword by
Taigen Dan Leighton.
    pages cm
  Includes bibliographical references.
  ISBN 1-61429-121-7 (pbk. : alk. paper)
  1. Shitou, 700–791. Cao an ge. 2. Spiritual life—Zen Buddhism. I. Title. II. Title:
Living Shitou's classic Zen poem.
  BQ9288.C66 2014
  294.3'444—dc23

                    2014000063



ISBN 9781614291213
eBook ISBN 9781614291442

19
5  4  3  2

Author photo courtesy of Dan Corrigan. The image on page ii is Shitou Xiqian,
from an 1880 wood-block print. Cover design by Phil Pascuzzo. Interior design by
Gopa&Ted2, Inc. Set in Requiem 10.9/15.8.

MIX
Paper from
responsible sources
FSC
www.fsc.org   FSC® C011935

For more information, please visit www.fscus.org.

# Table of Contents

# Foreword

BY TAIGEN DAN LEIGHTON

The important early Zen master Shitou is a major ancestor in the Chinese Caodong, or Japanese Soto, lineage—a lineage that is now very significant in the spread of Buddhism to the West. He is best known for his poem "Harmony of Difference and Sameness," or "Sandokai" in Japanese, which presented the underlying philosophy, imagery, and dialectical polarities foundational to all of Zen Buddhism but especially significant in the Caodong/Soto lineage. This poem by Shitou is a clear precursor for the poem "Song of the Jewel Mirror Samadhi," attributed to the lineage founder Dongshan in the following century.

Shitou is said to have lived from 700 to 790. His poem "Song of the Grass-Roof Hermitage," the central text for this book, presents not the philosophy of Zen, as "Harmony of Difference and Sameness" does, but instead offers a clear, helpful model for its actual practice, and for how to create a space of practice. Shitou built and resided in his grass-roof hermitage near his larger temple, where he trained numbers of students. His hut was his literal practice place, but it also serves as a metaphor for all Zen practice spaces. Lines from this "Song of the Grass-Roof Hermitage" are mentioned by later Soto figures such as Dongshan, Hongzhi, and Dogen and can be found embedded in koan collections such as the *Blue Cliff Record* and the *Book of Serenity*. But the poem as a whole was relatively neglected, certainly compared to the more celebrated "Harmony of Difference and Sameness." I came across some reference to the second poem in biographical materials about Shitou and translated it in 1985 together with my friend Kaz Tanahashi; it was first published by the *Windbell* journal of the San Francisco Zen Center.

I am very pleased that Ben Connelly has chosen to use Shitou's "Song of the Grass-Roof Hermitage" as an inspiration for his fine, personal practice reflections in this book. I am also very pleased that this poem is chanted at the Minnesota Zen Meditation Center where Ben practices, as it is in my temple in Chicago. This illuminating poem is now finally receiving some of the attention it richly deserves. It had not previously been part of any liturgy to my knowledge, and I am grateful to have helped promote its reemergence. Along with Ben I heartily recommend chanting the "Song of the Grass-Roof Hermitage"; my students have found it very inspiring.

A story about Shitou worth recounting relates that one of his main disciples once asked him about the essential meaning of Buddhadharma. Shitou responded, "Not to attain, not to know." The student then asked whether there was any other pivotal point, and Shitou said, "The wide sky does not obstruct the white clouds drifting." The flavor of Shitou's practice is not to worry about any attainment or accomplishment, or even to know anything. This is difficult for many contemporary students trained, in our acquisitive consumerist society, to accumulate accomplishments. Many students also think they need to figure out some rational understanding of Zen sayings. But as Shitou says about himself, "This mountain monk doesn't understand at all." Shitou encourages a spacious sense of practice, even in his small hut that includes the whole wide sky. But in this open-hearted space, the drifting clouds of practice are meaningful and not at all obstructed.

I especially appreciate Ben Connelly's taking on and opening up the many environmental implications of the "Song of the Grass-Roof Hermitage." Shitou realized that his hut, and each of our own spaces of practice, includes the entire world. We are each indeed deeply interconnected to the whole of nature. As Ben elaborates, Shitou's living lightly on the earth has major repercussions informing the Buddhist teaching of non-self, and how to see beyond our usual habitual grasping after self-identity.

I am tempted to comment myself on many of the numerous wonderful, rich lines in the "Song of the

Grass-Roof Hermitage." But I will leave that to Ben Connelly, and for the reader, to proceed. However, I must say that Shitou's "Turn around the light to shine within, then just return" marvelously contains all of Buddhist practice and its primary rhythm in one line. Further, Shitou's line "Let go of hundreds of years and relax completely" is a wonderful antidote to significant, harmful misunderstandings of Zen practice in our time. The point of Zen practice is to relieve suffering and promote liberation for all beings. Shitou tells us that the way to actively express such universal liberation involves relaxing completely. Please consider this thoroughly.

And please enjoy Shitou's song, and the many helpful harmonies that Ben Connelly has added for you.

*Taigen Leighton*
*September 2013*

---

Taigen Dan Leighton is the author of *Zen Questions: Zazen, Dogen, and the Spirit of Creative Inquiry* and *Faces of Compassion: Classic Bodhisattva Archetypes and Their Modern Expression*, as well as the cotranslator of *Dogen's Extensive Record*. He is the Dharma teacher at the Ancient Dragon Zen Gate in Chicago.

# Introduction

Thank you for being here with me. Through words, we can be together right now across space and time. Through this book, we can spend a little time with an old monk, his poem, a great tradition, and each other.

I encourage you to give yourself to this time. This particular moment is an opportunity for each of us to give our wholehearted attention to what is here: the air we breathe, the words we read, the sensations in our body, the sounds around us, and the activity of our minds and our hearts. This is a way of being to which we can always aspire.

Remember that turning your wholehearted attention to this text, or to whatever you happen to be doing, can be of benefit to every being—even if it's not obvious how. This may seem like a strange idea—or a very familiar one—but it is essential to the Buddhist tradition. Our study of the Dharma, and our practice of giving ourselves to each moment, should always be done with the intention to somehow lift the overall well-being of the world.

This book is not an attempt to explain the "Song of the Grass-Roof Hermitage." Instead, I write in order to engage my understanding with the text—in order to engage with your understanding. I meet the text with who I am and I invite you to meet Shitou's poem and my commentary with your own heart and mind. This is not about arriving at some kind of truth. Instead, it's about an interaction that is conducive to wellness and a friendly, open, and generous way of being. When we meet a teaching this way, our mind learns to meet life this way, and our actions flower out of this with a lightness, a freshness, a wisdom, and—most importantly—with kindness.

The historical record we have of Shitou Xiqian is sparse and lacking in many solid facts.

There is some evidence that he lived in the eighth century, in the heart of the great classical era of Chinese Zen. However, the details of these records are sufficiently divergent that piecing together much of a clear history is quite difficult. It appears he came to be called Shitou, or "stone top," after a shelf of stone on the mountain in southern China where he made his home late in life. The mountain was the site of a number of monasteries, being in a central region at a very fruitful time in the development of Zen, but Shitou's home was a small hut.

Shitou left us two poems, each of about two hundred Chinese characters: "Harmony of Difference and Sameness" and the "Song of the Grass-Roof Hermitage." The first is widely used as a teaching vehicle, particularly in Soto Zen circles. Its subject is, in broadest terms, the relationship between the absolute and the relative aspects of things. If that sounds a little abstruse, it is. However, these were central ideas used in the practice of Chinese Zen and are still valuable subjects for inquiry.

I love both of Shitou's poems; however, "Song of the Grass-Roof Hermitage" seems to me to be of particular resonance for our times. Living lightly on the land, calmly and happily; letting go of whatever blocks us from being available to those around us; patient devotion to peace—these are themes that are worth coming back to again and again. Shitou manages to teach complex Buddhist ideas in this poem without resorting to the technical language that makes many classic texts inaccessible to the general reader; its simple imagery and tone evoke a calm, relaxed, and open approach to things. This is a poem written by a Zen monk, but it avoids sectarian clichés. Its teachings are therefore much more accessible to Western Buddhists, who are in the process of forming a new tradition of practice from elements of the entire range and history of pan-Asian Buddhist teachings.

There are two principal strains of Chinese Zen poems. Some are very oriented toward teaching, such as Sengcan's "Heart Mind Inscription," and some are more personal expressions of the author's immediate experience, usually focusing on detailed depictions of the natural world. The works of Cold Mountain and Stonehouse come to mind as examples of the latter. The "Song of the Grass-Roof Hermitage" bridges these types; it gives numerous clear practice instructions and alludes to a comprehensive array of the central matters of Buddhism, but it also depicts in natural imagery a simple life of ease and compassion. For a teaching poem it is a work of remarkable literary merit—it is beautiful, and I think we could all use a little beauty. The fact that this work calls itself a "song" evokes something lovely, though I know of no melody or music that was ever a part of it. I encourage you to listen for the music of the language, for the melody in Taigen Leighton's lovely, lyrical translation.

This poem, like most Chinese Zen texts, invites an enormous array of interpretations; a single Chinese character can allude to numerous (sometimes opposing) meanings, stories, and other teachings. The approach I've taken is to expand a bit on the poem's description of a life of simple practice and to talk about the many elements of the thousand years of Buddhist thought alluded to—and then to show how we can manifest the poem's principles in our lives. Each chapter in this book is a response to a single line of the poem and expands upon a key theme the line presents. As a whole the chapters together present what I hope is a fairly complete engagement with the poem's teachings.

This book is intended to support and encourage Buddhist practice, which is, in essence, meditation and kind actions. If you are reading this book to acquire knowledge, that is good, but I hope that you will consider doing so to be part of a practice whose purpose is the alleviation of suffering—that you will frame this action in the context of this simple purpose for which Buddhism exists. Throughout the text there are references to meditation practice. I will be frank: reading this book is not a substitute for meditation practice. However, both in combination is quite wonderful; textual study and meditation have been integral parts of the Buddhist tradition for as long as it's been around. If you are looking for reasons or encouragement to meditate, or supplements to aid your practice, read on. I wrote this book because I care about you, your family, the people in your neighborhood, your country, the world, and all the ants, grass, and fishes. More than anything, I hope it helps you to be kind.

# A Note on Chanting and Recitation

In every culture people come together to sing. In churches, at concert halls, amid the roar of electric guitars in basements, on playgrounds, and in nursing homes. All over the world people recite poems and prayers together. Although it is no longer as common in the United States as it once was, children all over the world still learn by rote memorization; their high, singsong voices roving through words and rhythms that have been repeated and passed down for generations. These are ways of connecting thought, culture, and behavior that create a sense of togetherness and develop the capacities of memory and concentration. Buddhist teachings were originally passed down exclusively in this manner; the Buddha and his contemporaries had no written language, so the teachings we have were passed along for hundreds of years through recitation and chanting, until they were at last written down.

In Asian Buddhism chanting is a basic part of the practice; the words of the tradition are accompanied and supported with very simple pitched and rhythmic singing. In the United States, the role of chanting varies, as sanghas construct their own modes of practice, assimilating, adapting, and discarding aspects of Asian Buddhism. I have visited American practice centers where chanting was a daily occurrence and others where no chanting was ever done. Some people I know think that chanting and other ritual aspects that come to us from Asia are crucial; others think they are not helpful at all. Many of us are in the middle on this question. One friend is opposed to chanting Zen texts in the traditional manner but encourages reciting them; for some reason not having a sung pitch seems right to him. Another friend told me of visiting a place where the chanting sounded too much like a song because it had a flowing melody. She said it felt like church, so she never returned. There are complex reasons people have such reactions and opinions, and since I want to encourage you recite or chant the "Song of the Grass-Roof Hermitage," I thought I'd better let you know you're not alone if you have some opinions about it. I encourage an open, inquisitive mind and being aware of the thoughts and feelings that arise on this subject.

I think chanting or reciting texts that promote our welfare is an excellent practice, and I encourage you to take it up. The "Song of the Grass-Roof Hermitage" is a wonderful one to start with. It's lovely, and it encourages peace of mind. If you'd like to chant you can just sing each syllable on a single pitch; just pick a note and don't change it. If you'd like to recite, just read in a relaxed voice and cadence. Don't stop to think about the words—just let the experience of making and hearing the sounds be the focus of your attention. Feel your body producing sound; feel the emotional impact on your body as you produce the words. This is a practice of deep listening as much as it is a practice of producing sound. Right before or after a period of meditation—and right before or right after reading a chapter of this book—is a perfect time to do this. The poem takes about two minutes to chant.

These voiced ways of relating to a text bring it into your body and your senses; they draw your relationship to the text into a wider field of your consciousness than just your cognitive mind. They'll bring it into your body, your ears, and into your heart. They bring kind and loving speech onto your lips and tongue and draw it up from your breath. They promote concentration, so central to Buddha's vision for a path to liberation. Sounding these words out loud connects you to thousands of years and millions of lives of Buddhist practice, of countless voices offering themselves to the possibility of peace and harmony.

·

# 石头草庵歌

吾结草庵无宝贝、饭了从容图睡快。

成时初见茆草新、破後还将茆草盖。

住庵人、镇常在。不属中间与内外。

世人住处我不住、世人爱处我不爱。

庵虽小、含法界。方丈老人相体解。

上乘菩萨信无疑、中下闻之必生怪。

问此庵、坏不坏。坏与不坏主元在。

不居南北与东西、基址坚牢以为最。

青松下、明窗内。玉殿朱楼未为对。

衲帔幪头万事休、此时山僧都不会。

住此庵、休作解。谁夸铺席图人买。

回光返照便归来、廓达灵根非向背。

遇祖师、亲训诲。结草为庵莫生退。

百年抛却任纵横、摆手便行且无罪。

千种言、万般解。只要教君长不昧。

欲识庵中不死人、岂离而今这皮袋。

# Song of the Grass-Roof Hermitage

## SHITOU (700–790)

Translated by Taigen Dan Leighton
and Kazuaki Tanahashi

I've built a grass hut where there's nothing of value.
After eating, I relax and enjoy a nap.
When it was completed, fresh weeds appeared.
Now it's been lived in—covered by weeds.

The person in the hut lives here calmly,
Not stuck to inside, outside, or in between.
Places worldly people live, he doesn't live.
Realms worldly people love, he doesn't love.

Though the hut is small, it includes the entire world.
In ten feet square, an old man illumines forms and
   their nature.
A Great Vehicle bodhisattva trusts without doubt.
The middling or lowly can't help wondering;
Will this hut perish or not?

Perishable or not, the original master is present,
Not dwelling south or north, east or west.
Firmly based on steadiness, it can't be surpassed.
A shining window below the green pines—
Jade palaces or vermilion towers can't compare with it.

Just sitting with head covered, all things are at rest.
Thus, this mountain monk doesn't understand at all.
Living here he no longer works to get free.
Who would proudly arrange seats, trying to entice
    guests?

Turn around the light to shine within, then just return.
The vast inconceivable source can't be faced or turned
    away from.
Meet the ancestral teachers, be familiar with their
    instruction,
Bind grasses to build a hut, and don't give up.

Let go of hundreds of years and relax completely.
Open your hands and walk, innocent.
Thousands of words, myriad interpretations,
Are only to free you from obstructions.
If you want to know the undying person in the hut,
Don't separate from this skin bag here and now.

# 1

## Living Simply in the Changes

I'VE BUILT A GRASS HUT WHERE THERE'S
NOTHING OF VALUE.

## THINGS CHANGE

A grass hut is a home but not a very durable one, especially considering it was built in an era when great
pagodas were constructed and in a culture that formed
an immense wall of stone, thousands of miles long. A
storm could surely reduce it to a thin green veil disap-
pearing in the wind. Our poet Shitou is inviting us into
his home, and this is the kind of home he built: one that
makes the absolute minimum claim to permanence.

The earliest Buddhist teachings continually point us
toward the subject of impermanence, of facing this reality. As Buddha said, "Everything that comes to be must
pass away; make your peace with this and all will be well."
Suffering arises from trying to turn away from impermanence; liberation arises from facing it fully. It was the
pain of seeing the suffering at the end of life, of sick-
ness, of old age, and of death that motivated Siddhartha

Gotama to pursue his quest for liberation. His teachings say that directly engaging with this most difficult aspect of human existence is the way to let go of, or hold more lightly, both the small day-to-day aggravations and the wrenching, life-changing griefs: struggling to make deadlines, arguing with a child, spilling our coffee, profound illnesses, and the loss of our loved ones' lives. Though this is a poem that describes a life of profound ease and moment-to-moment engagement with life, it starts not by saying our poet has built a perfect sanctuary but that he is instead simply living with uncertainty.

Can you think of something permanent? Is there anything that has always been and will always be? Anything that has come into being that will never change? I cannot find anything that fits this description. Sometimes I think that the total dynamic activity of all energy and matter that has ever been goes on forever, but I really don't know if it will or if it ever actually "began." I can't see those end points. If I use my senses, my eyes, my nose, my ears, my tongue, my body, my mind, I cannot find anything that is permanent. I can *imagine* things and I know many believe in things such as an everlasting God, but I do not *know* if such exists. I know that when I observe, what appears before me is change.

I own a big house in south Minneapolis. It's always in the process of falling apart. I go out in the yard and pick up chunks of siding that blew off in the wind. I had to replace the water heater a while back. Sometimes I experience unhappiness when yet another part of this house falls off, but really it's a guarantee: our stuff falls apart. And when it happens, that's just the world doing what it does. As my teacher Tim Burkett recently said, "If your bodies weren't falling apart you'd be dead. Who came up with this system?!" We don't like it, but here it is. This book is not going to be about a fairy land, or take you to someplace where everything is perfect; Buddhism is not a tradition about going to some other place where things are how we like them. We're getting a invitation into this little hut, it's got a stone slab floor with some ragged reed mats, we'll probably have to rebuild it next year, and it's long, long gone thirteen hundred years after this poem was written.

Shitou builds a grass hut to encourage us to let go of the story that we can somehow go against the fundamental fact that nothing lasts and everything is always changing. Our minds are conditioned to relentlessly tell us this story. I bought a nice big house and it cost a lot of money; shouldn't it provide security? We might not phrase the question this way, but when we are upset this is the underlying message on which our mind operates. Really, when the pipes burst and water is spraying around the kitchen, how often do we operate from the understanding that this is a natural part of the process of change? We sometimes do experience and live from this understanding, and sometimes it happens spontaneously, but for most of us it takes practice. This book is about that practice that promotes living fully engaged with change.

How many times has something ended that you enjoyed, and so you found yourself suffering? When the lunch break with friends ends, and you find yourself back at work watching the clock? When a lover leaves you? When death comes and takes away the mother that you love so much or perhaps with whom things have always been so hard? This always-endingness of things is hard to take, and Shitou begins by saying, "I am accepting it; I am going to sit right down in this impermanence. This is where I make my home, in a hut of grass: permeable, ephemeral." This is not a metaphorical hut. It's a little house. It's green. It's sitting on the side of a small, lush mountain in China, and inside is an old man who says, "Come in, I've made this choice to live in and with the inexorability of change and I would like to tell you a bit about how this is, and how it is so very good; please join me."

## LIVING LIGHTLY ON THE LAND

Houses of wood were popular when this poem was written, and we still frame houses with wood today. They can stand for hundreds of years; most of our houses these days have as their bones dead trees.

Buildings made of stone, of course, last even longer; you can find stone structures in China and across the world that have been standing for thousands of years. Stone, though, must be quarried from the earth and transported with immense human effort. You can see the deep cuts made in the earth from quarrying for many, many years. Similarly, near my mother's mountain home, we drive through long stretches of clear-cut forest, where stumps and low grass occupy a land once home to thousands of immense, old, and living beings. Grass, on the other hand, is quite a thing; cut it, and it grows right back. Incredibly resilient, it is a basic wellspring of life for vast tracts of land across the earth where millions of grazers eat grass—and grass just keeps growing. Living in a grass hut is a way to avoid leaving big scars on the earth, to avoid laying waste to lots of life, but still have just enough protection while living with the renewable resources the land provides.

Where I live, a grass home doesn't sound so good. The lovely summer months in Minnesota end, and the winter is very cold, with many feet of snowfall. People grimace as they fight the ice on the windshields of their cars, making only brief appearances in the outdoors—spending the rest of their time in their large buildings that are heated by petroleum products dug from deep in the earth and transported halfway around the world, or in their three-thousand-pound metal transportation devices powered by the same fuels. Grass hut indeed. Sure, Shitou did not live in Minnesota. However, the Lakota and Ojibwe lived here for thousands of years with homes made of animal hide. These are people who saw constantly renewing abundance where we tend to see scarcity.

In the summer I take backpacking trips in the mountains with my family, and in the last few years, I've begun to bring people backpacking on silent meditation retreats. Cutting down on the things you have does something good for the mind. When you spend several days, or weeks, with the necessities of your life all in a single bag on your back, you get a little closer to the basics of life. You use less and you know exactly what you're using. When you carry the garbage you create with you around for a few days, until you leave the wilderness and put it in a garbage can, you see a basic truth—there is not really an *away* where you can throw things. You become a little more intimate with what you consume. When we spend time deep in the woods we see how much more vast and dynamic nature is than anything we could construct, but we also see how easy it would be for us to denude it in order to extract things we want. We see something whose preciousness is dependent on us letting it be.

The earliest Buddhist monks lived very lightly on the land; they had no homes, they ate little, and they wore discarded rags. These practices were not motivated by an altruistic love for the earth—the Buddha taught that renunciation of worldly goods was the best way to be free from suffering. Wanting and gaining material things is an extraordinarily ineffective means of promoting our welfare, but our culture keeps pushing us to do it. The results are not going well for the other species on our planet, and they are not going well for our children and grandchildren. How can we live in a way where we see that what the earth naturally and renewably provides is enough? How can we manifest the wisdom of living in a hut of grass that will blow away and grow right back?

I live in a wood-frame house, and I will be quite surprised if anyone reading this book decides to move into a grass hut, but this poem has encouraged me to look at what I consume and why. Changing my habits to consume less and have a less-damaging impact on the world is a process for me. I stopped eating meat a while back, shortly after I was ordained as a Zen priest. I chose to do so not because of rules, but because I am encouraged to be inquisitive about how my actions affect others. I get more vegetables from local farms; I keep looking for ways to walk and bike more and drive less. I'm not here to tell you what to do, but I encourage you to be attentive to what you're using and how it affects you and everything else. This poem's message of a life of ease starts with an image of relying on the renewable resources the world offers and letting go of all the fancy things we can buy. It is showing how little you need to be well. It's showing that abundance is here when we keep it simple, and scarcity is here when we want more.

## NOTHING OF VALUE

There's nothing of value here in this grass hut: no cash, no fancy clothes, no jewels. The monk makes a place where those things we desire are not; this withdrawal from the surface pleasures of the material world has been part of many spiritual practices. Sometimes this austerity seems difficult and we feel deprived, at other times we realize the total freedom it offers. There have been times during meditation-intensive Zen retreats where the simplicity and austerity of our practice seemed totally barren and I longed for a malted milk, a good book, or the arms of my beloved, and there have been times when my gratitude for just the opportunity to be alive in this moment with nothing but a warm place to sit and the sound of the birds inside the stillness was so very vast. This vast spaciousness is not so easy to find when we are surrounded with our usual array of possessions. So our mountain monk makes his home without them.

Although this hut is just a humble home, it's also a symbol for the mind. Shitou's abode is the hut he built, as well as the mind he trained. Sitting in meditation and leaving behind the focus on material pleasures allows the mind to slow down and take a break from deciding what it wants and what it doesn't, to become a mind where there's nothing of value. A mind where all things are equal, a mind at peace. When we value something there is always comparison, always something we don't want. Experiment: Think of something that has value to you and start looking around. Do you value everything equally? Your phone, your favorite book, your hands, the sounds you are hearing right now, the flu, the dust under the couch? Ascribing value is essentially the source of the suffering that the most basic teaching of Buddhism offers to transcend. We ascribe a positive value to something, generally totally unconsciously, and feel attached to it, and when it is not there we suffer. We ascribe negative value to something else, feel aversion, and suffer from the object's presence. It is possible, according to the teaching of Shakyamuni Buddha, to cease to suffer from attachment and aversion; he shows how to find a mind where there is no valuation, where all things are equal, where there is nothing of value.

Of course, the capacity to discern good and bad, and realize that feeding our hungry baby is more important than gazing at sparkling dust motes in the morning sun, is important and necessary, but when it is supported by the capacity to just let things be without judging, lots of room opens up. We can experience the sparkling dust completely and take care of our loved ones whole-heartedly too. This mind, which is free from value, is not apathetic. If you have two hungry children, one of whom you like and one you find annoying, would you give the one you prefer more food? This is about letting go of judgments in this moment and finding a helpful heart.

The contents of this hut are nothing of value, which is to say, not valuing things is not of value. Our monk does not claim to have made a place where he has moved beyond valuing things, for then he would have acquired a fantastic treasure, to which he would surely be very attached. He is not claiming or offering any magical teachings or infinite wisdom. He has not invited you into his mountainside home to show you that he has some incredibly special enlightenment. He invites you in and says there's nothing of value you here, nothing special. He is making a humble offering. He has invited you into this simple place to give you a space to let go of wanting—wanting things, wanting spiritual achievements, wanting peace of mind—to let go of the endless separation of yourself from this infinitely unfolding shapeshiftingness by relinquishing picking and choosing. This is an invitation to just be completely here.

# 2

## Enjoying the Middle Way

AFTER EATING, I RELAX AND ENJOY A NAP.

## THE MIDDLE WAY

According to the oldest records of the Buddhist tradition, the first teaching Buddha gave after his great enlightenment was on the practice of the Middle Way: the path between the one extreme of hardcore asceticism, which tries to rise above suffering by denying our bodies, and the other extreme of hedonism, which tries to deal with suffering by indulging our endless desires. Having tried both methods and been unsatisfied, he arrived at this Middle as the way to deep peace. This is a way where we eat enough to be well, we take care of our bodies, we don't take any more than we need, and we practice meditation and active kindness. I'm afraid, though, that the Buddha's understanding of this Middle Way probably sounds incredibly ascetic to our modern ears. He advised leaving home and family, giving up all material possessions except what you could easily carry with you, not eating after noon, only eating food that was given to you... the list goes on. On the plus side, contrary to some popular ascetic practices in India at the time, he did invite people to eat enough to be healthy and to skip undertaking the practice of ceasing to breathe. So, like Buddha's friends at rest in the shifting patches of shade in the Jetta Grove, don't feel overly indulgent if you take a deep breath right now and experience it with your whole being.

The way we practice today is not the ancient way. The methods of practice, of walking this Middle Way, have changed and today most of us have homes, people who are dear to us, and a host of possessions. The Way isn't always clear. The Middle is not a definite location; it can't be found in a time or in a single teaching. We must simply strive toward being open to what is, regardless of the circumstances.

Shitou is reminding us of an old Zen saying on the Middle Way: "When you are hungry, eat. When you are tired, sleep." He's not sitting on his meditation cushion until it turns into a diamond; he's enjoying a nap. Just look, an old man at peace in a grass shack on a sunshine-dappled mountainside. Arguably the most consistent theme of this poem is "Relax." I encourage you to read through the poem and find these words and phrases: "relax, calmly, at rest, relax completely, open your hands." This is an invitation to be at ease.

Shitou shows us a picture of his practice; he builds something small, fragile, and unimposing and is at rest. What a humble view of the activity of one of the great, celebrated sages of his time! What a small, simple expression of humanity from one whose poetic work profoundly touches countless lives. Can we remember this Middle Way of building a house, taking care of our bodies, and being at ease? Can we work, be healthy and calm, and enjoy the simplicity of things as it is? Can we devote ourselves to making a beautiful contribution to the world and do it with humility? Shitou gave us this poem, and he gave us his little green hut. What is your Middle Way? I would love to know how you give to the world and to hear about how you can work with a sense of ease.

We're not in the Middle if we just bliss out and ignore all the suffering in the world. What about the poor, what about the children, what about the pollutants and the wars, my aging mom, and my struggling teenage child? What about my own aching heart? Let's remember the context; this poem is about being in his little grass hut, a place where our teacher has retreated to devote himself to practice and simple life. He also spent many years writing and teaching people how to be well and kind. He found a Middle Way between retreat from and engagement with the world. His life was devoted to the alleviation of suffering and that devotion took many forms. I believe this: we need to retreat, we need to spend time being simple and focusing on being at ease in the moment, in order to fully manifest our capacity to be of service. You can retreat to a hermitage, or with a meditation community, or you can retreat to a walk around the block when you are so mad at your family that you want to weep with frustration, you can retreat to three mindful breaths as you look up from the hours we spend gazing at glowing screens. The most basic retreat Zen recommends is the retreat to sitting meditation, what Dogen Zenji calls "the Dharma gate of joy and ease."

Sometimes it isn't easy to find the time to meditate, or do something helpful, or be at ease. There is a discipline to ease; Shitou's having a nap. Sleep is very important. Most Americans don't get enough, so we're frazzled. There is a day-to-day discipline of taking care of this body and a day-to-day discipline of getting to the cushion to meditate. For me, the strict and challenging discipline of Zen meditation retreats has opened up a realm and life of ease I did not realize was possible. It's good to be disciplined about taking it easy, to walk a Middle Way between doing practice to cultivate our capacity for ease and just being at ease with what is right now.

## ENJOYMENT

I will make an embarrassing confession. When I was in the sixth grade, in a school bound by cornfields, my little orange notebooks were scrawled with the phrase "peace love 'n joy." Oh, how my older brother loved to tease me for that 'n. Perhaps I have missed my calling in the usage of nonstandard conjunctions and I should be naming plastic-roofed restaurants for the lining of American freeways. I am bemused, though, at how much I still value these simple qualities: peace, love, AND joy. Perhaps I should here too confess that, between the sixth grade and my late twenties, there was a long period where my interest in these qualities steadily declined as I descended into darker and darker levels of drug and alcohol addiction, addictions from which I have experienced freedom now for many years. In this freedom I have found my values have become brighter and clearer to me—and among these surely resides joy, or enjoyment.

Enjoyment is not such a simple theme in the Buddhist tradition. The earliest Buddhist teachings generally point toward letting go of enjoyment, for the simple reason that it leads to attachment. Some devotees of this earliest style seem to be really sorry to see a potentially huge failing in the nascent tradition of Western Buddhism; by emphasizing mindfulness and the enjoyment of whatever present-moment phenomena are arising, are people just learning to be attached to immediate sense pleasure? How could that be the way to nirvana, the cessation of suffering that arises from attachment and aversion? If you read the Four Foundations of

Mindfulness Sutra, one of the seminal early Buddhist texts, you will definitely not find anything about having a mindful meal and completely experiencing and enjoying each sensation. You will instead find a long series of visualization exercises picturing different stages of the decomposition of one's body after death. The Buddha was a really challenging teacher.

My personal experience with Zen practice certainly highlights this matter. Regularly practicing meditation and mindfulness cause the categories of what you enjoy to expand and the separation from your life caused by ceaseless mental activity to fade. Many are the times when, after doing some sitting meditation, I step outside of the zendo and find myself joyously attuned to the sounds of the many birds in chorus, simply standing still and enjoying the slow shifting and waving of the boughs and leaves of the great trees that line the lake. It's very hard for me to conceptualize this as a bad thing.

Perhaps this is because the practice of mindfulness that I do is a part of a broader Zen practice that includes vows to be kind, cultivation of awareness of my emotional reactivity, study of how attachment causes suffering, community service, manual labor, examination of Buddhist texts, deep meditative states during long retreats, and support from my teacher and all my wonderful friends. Somehow when you put this all together something very interesting happens with this enjoyment of the present moment. We start to enjoy things that seem way outside of what we expect to find enjoyable. I recall one time when two loved ones were bickering vociferously when getting ready for a family party. They fight with frequency and it's clear after many years of knowing them that it's not helpful for me to directly intervene. I recall sweeping the floors and enjoying the feel of the broom in my hand, the steady accumulation of detritus in little piles, and the shrill sound of the two people arguing—and feeling a still, quiet joy, love, and appreciation for them just as they were at that time, a tenderness toward them in their immediate suffering. I'd check in occasionally to ask what I could do to help get ready and then return to the work. Considering the fact that historically I have really disliked housework and tend to be very emotionally reactive to conflict, this experience seemed pretty extraordinary. I hope the calm I brought helped my two dear family members, and I am beyond grateful to all who have supported me in this practice that made such enjoyment possible.

A balance exists between accidently cultivating attachment by being present to life and denying oneself the enjoyment of your moments as a means to let go of attachment; it is a Middle Way between realizing impermanence and realizing the present moment. The earliest Buddhist teachings include practices to concentrate the mind on present-moment phenomena and also practices to remind us of the inevitability of death and the dissolution of all things, including ourselves and loved ones. (I'll leave it to you to guess which practices are most popular.) But here we're talking of Shitou, and he gives us the very same Middle Way. The old man builds a flimsy, impermanent hut of grass and branches as his dwelling on the side of a mountain, whose weather is more vast and unpredictable than any tiny human effort, and in that full offering of himself to impermanence he enjoys being at rest.

# 3

## Unwithering Fertility

WHEN IT WAS COMPLETED,
FRESH WEEDS APPEARED.

My friend Ted likes weeding. He likes to kneel down in the dirt and carefully and attentively pull up the plants that are not wanted, to leave room for others. I have seen him quietly contributing to the growth of many green beings by pulling handfuls up by their dirt-trailing roots. This is a job that he knows has no end, for weeds will keep growing.

Gardening is a well-worn symbol for the meditation process, for the Buddhist process of cultivating a mind free from suffering. We sometimes say we water the seeds of good in our mind and we pull up the roots of harmful tendencies. This is a metaphorical expression for right effort, the sixth element of the Noble Eightfold Path. In less poetic terms, the Nikayas define right effort as the endeavor to cultivate and sustain wholesome mind-states and let go of unwholesome ones; the term "right" in the Eightfold Path means conducive to well-being rather than referring to some kind of absolute moral value. Right effort is very good practice if it's done with lots of compassion for ourselves, help from our friends, and mindful attention. But it can be limiting; the other meditative elements of the Eightfold Path—right mindfulness and right concentration—allow us to just simply, openly, nonjudgmentally, and without ascribing value see what's growing, what's here. This view can help us realize that we are the weeds and flowers and that the weeds and flowers are the whole world.

Lots of people who come to our center to learn how to meditate say after the first few times, "I can't do it; I'm always distracted." I'm sympathetic; it's kind of a drag to realize so quickly just how absurdly dominating our cognitive function is. We sit down in a room together, the teacher slowly talks through some calming and focusing words, he or she rings a bell, and... thoughts. Fresh weeds appear. That's what they do. Wow! Look at them: slim leaves, broad leaves, tiny flowers or large, smooth and spiny, the rich earthy scent of catsfoot. Who could call these weeds? We call them weeds when we don't like them; when we are mindful, we just see them as they are, in all their vividness.

Fresh weeds appear, but often we meditators don't want the weeds, we want the cleared-out garden with just what we planted, we want a different garden than the one that's here. Right effort can seem to make a lot of sense. In right effort I know what to do: "I'm going to get rid of this bad stuff in my mind and make some more good stuff." It's a pretty conventional way of being—picking and choosing what we want and don't. This isn't necessarily bad; it's just really limited. Right mindfulness and right concentration allow us to taste and see the endlessly growing, vastly nuanced, incomprehensibly interdependent garden that we're usually missing because we're trying to narrow it down into something we can figure out and arrange according to our own personal tastes. So we let right effort be the small part of our practice—we let trying to control the mind be a small part of our practice—and let being mindful of the mind that is here be a big part, be a big mind.

Fresh weeds appear, this we can see, and our practice allows an opportunity to find a balance in how we treat them. Sometimes being with the weeds is simply accepting and appreciating the volunteer flowers that show up unexpectedly. We don't have to water them. We don't have to pick them and make a bouquet to carry with us. We can just let them be and let them go. Sometimes being with the weeds is pulling those plants up, attentively, with our raw, dirt-blacked hands, so we can grow some flowers for all the passersby to enjoy, to bring them some beauty they may not even notice but whose presence requires infinite interdependence and a few drops of wholehearted human effort.

# 4

## Here with the Weeds

NOW IT'S BEEN LIVED IN—COVERED BY WEEDS.

Shitou begins our poem by saying there's nothing of value in his hut, but this going-beyond-value is the jewel of the Buddha's house. To have a mind that just meets each thing without deciding whether it is worthy or not, that meets everyone and everything just as it is, is realization. Shitou points toward something beyond description: the mind of enlightenment. He uses the humblest possible terms to describe what is held in the highest position by countless Buddhist texts. Having completed the Way, accomplished realization, tasted the truth that is beyond true and false, and gone beyond picking and choosing, what happened to our poet? His hut is covered by weeds. Shitou hasn't created a pure, weed-free realm. He's here with what keeps coming up. This is the tradition I choose to be a part of—not one where we practice to attain a permanent transcendence of suffering, but one where we practice to be here with the weeds.

Some would argue that the earliest Buddhist texts do teach us to train the mind so that it is no longer a place where suffering occurs, where there are no weeds, and that it's only the later Mahayana teachings that instruct us to allow the mind to soften to the point where we are simply not caught by our suffering, so that we may be available and helpful to all the world, so that we may be intimate with all the weeds. It's good to remember that all the records show Buddha spending his entire life helping anyone who came to him. Every kind of Buddhist teaching, no matter the tradition, is centered in alleviating suffering by being available to what is.

There are certainly a wide variety of Buddhist texts that suggest that a person can attain a complete and final cessation of suffering. If I experience this, I doubt that I will complain about it, and if you have, that is wonderful. However, this is not something I aspire to, and no one I know claims to have experienced it. For me, practice is about cultivating the capacity to alleviate suffering. There is no end point, just an endlessly manifesting vow to offer each moment to the well-being of all things.

This line of verse is sly. Is our narrator a little cranky that his place is covered by weeds? Or does he think it's lovely? Because he doesn't tell us, there is room for us to enter this line and see that our attitude toward what comes up makes all the difference. Sometimes here in Minnesota we get great heaps of snow in late April when we expect spring. I hear a lot of complaining. I also know one or two people who get really excited: "It's SO beautiful!" I try to appreciate the conditions outside (which I rather enjoy) and also appreciate the feelings of the people who talk to me about it. I direct energy to wholeheartedly being with what's here, whether it's the weather or people's dissatisfaction. When Shitou built the hut he didn't expect the weeds, and when we made it through winter we didn't expect the extra snow, but our expectations don't have much impact on the fact that weeds and snow appear.

Rather than building a house and scrupulously keeping it clean, Shitou builds a hut and lets the weeds that climb and cover the mountainside swallow it up. He does not create a barrier between himself and all the woes of the world; he lives right inside them without getting caught up. And if sometimes he complains—"Covered by weeds!"—he shows us that being there with that complaint is just a part of being with the weeds, a part of his life, a part of his practice.

Dainin Katagiri, who brought Zen to Minnesota many years ago, is buried high on a hill at the wooded rural Zen practice center Hokyoji. There is a beautiful well-kept stone monument there and, leading up to it, a series of cobblestone steps. The devoted community at Hokyoji keeps that gravesite clean and lovely, but there is no way to keep the weeds of the great wilds of Hokyoji from springing up between the cobbles. I like to think that we honor our teacher and tradition by keeping the grave pristine—and also by letting the weeds among the stones that lead us there live their green and precious lives.

# 5

## Who Is This Person?

In the first lines of this poem, we are given a first-person narrator: "I've built a grass hut where there's nothing of value. After eating, I relax and enjoy a nap." Now we are told, "the person in the hut lives here calmly." Where did our first person go? Chinese is a language where ambiguity regarding pronouns can be very easily achieved, but the Chinese characters in Shitou's poem use specific language to move from the "I" to "the person." So I'm left wondering, "Who is this person?" Is it Shitou? Is it a fictional mountain dweller? Is it me, is it you, is it all of us? Who is this person?

In simplest terms we could say that this moving from the first to the third person points to a letting go of attachment to the self—a big topic for the Buddha. One of his main insights was that he couldn't locate anything that actually was him, his, or his self. This is an observation with profound metaphysical implications that are celebrated in later Buddhist teachings, but what is most wonderful to me is the practicality of it. In the earliest records of Buddhism, he says that thinking that anything is you, yours, or yourself causes suffering through attachment and thus makes no sense. He advises us to practice saying, "This body is not me, this body is not mine, this body is not myself. This feeling is not me, this feeling is not mine, this feeling is not myself. This thought is not..." etc. He doesn't try and prove some fundamental truth about nonself; he just shows a practical means to be well: by shedding conceptions of self hood.

So moving from the first person to the third in this poem is about moving to a state of wellness, of calm abiding. You can use the method Buddha advised above. Another practice to let go of being stuck on self is to refer to things you'd usually call "mine" as "the." For example: "the" body instead of "my" body, "the" mind instead of "my" mind, "the" computer instead of "my" computer. I caught myself recently when coordinating the staff for a retreat referring to the person who would serve as timekeeper as "my timekeeper." I could feel how that way of framing the role and my relationship to it heightened my sense of self, of importance, of grandiosity, so I've taken up the practice of being attentive to that linguistic tendency and the feelings and thoughts that arise with it.

Despite all my meditation practice, I can't find anything that is "my self," but it sure tends to seem to me like there is one. Through many hours of sitting still with the soft sighing of breath and the dull, textured roar of planes overhead, sensations in aching limbs slowly fading, things seem to arise and fade away. I can't say the body is mine, or the sounds, or the breath, or the thoughts, but still a little something usually seems to say, "I." This is probably ok, because "I" have to get home after the retreat and mow the lawn. And I've got Shitou to help me be okay with this, because it is an "I" that builds that little hut, and an "I" that takes a nap.

Between this "I" and "this person," between this sense we have that a self and this awareness of nonself, some space opens up. A little room for not-knowing. Isn't that what a zendo is, what your meditation cushion is, your yoga mat? Really, this little moment of consciousness right now is a small space for not-knowing. Here is an opportunity to let go of being absorbed in your preconceptions about yourself and ask, "Who is this person?"

We may think we know ourselves, but is it so? For instance, I always hated sewing and found it an exercise in intense shame-wracked frustration, so when I learned that to undergo a Zen initiation ceremony with Tim Burkett we had to sew a ritual garment, or *rakusu*, under the instruction of a Zen sewing master, the dear and wonderful Tomoe Katagiri, I knew I'd found a good practice. An opportunity to investigate the idea I had that "I" "hate" "sewing." I gave myself to the practice of mindful sewing and, lo and behold, although tears were shed and swears were sworn, I saw through some of that "I," and that "hate," and that "sewing." Who is the person I call "I"? What is this experience I call "hate"? What is this activity I call "sewing"? When you're faced with a task you know you don't like, can you ask yourself "Who is this person?" instead of knowing already? When you're stepping out the door for work, can you have some curiosity about who is going out? When you find yourself thinking "I hate that guy," can you ask, "Who is this person that's hating?" You can open your heart to yourself by showing a little curiosity.

I'm looking out at you across this keyboard, amid the buzz of power tools the neighbors are using and a very subtle breeze coming through the window, and I'm wondering, who is this person?

# 6

## Cultivating the Way, Inside and Out

NOT STUCK TO INSIDE, OUTSIDE, OR IN BETWEEN.

### ZEN AND YOGACARA

Yogacara is one of the many schools of Buddhist thought and practice that profoundly influenced and permeates Zen. Yogacara, which literally means "one who practices yoga," is also sometimes known as Vijnanavada, or Consciousness-Only Buddhism. One of the facets of this line, "Not stuck to inside, outside, or in between," is reflecting the lovely light of Yogacara on us right now.

In the fourth century, one of the great figures of Yogacara Buddhism, Vasubandhu, wrote the seminal "Thirty Verses on Consciousness-Only," a work that brought many diverging strains of Buddhist and yogic thought into a compact and coherent poem. I have memorized and chanted this poem regularly for years, after being inspired to taste its beauty and insight by reading Thich Nhat Hanh's recollection of being required to chant and memorize it, with all his fellows, when he was a young Zen monk in Vietnam. These verses were likely chanted by monks in Shitou's time, just as his "Song" is chanted now, and their wisdom shines throughout Zen literature. Sitting under a tree in the evening sunlight, quietly intoning the ancient words and feeling a deep connection to the generations of monks across the world who've done the same, is a truly lovely experience.

These "Thirty Verses" reconcile the emphasis in early Buddhism on transforming consciousness from something that experiences suffering into something that does not, with the later Mahayana focus on devotion to the nonconceptualized, unknowable, undivided emptiness that is ever-present, infinite compassion, inherently free but not separate from suffering. Early Buddhism stresses looking inward at consciousness itself; Mahayana underlines seeing that inside and outside are not two separate things. And conventional human thought advises judging and manipulating apparently external objects in order to get what you want. So when old Shitou says, "Not stuck to inside, outside, or in between," he is calling us back to Yogacara and telling us to not get stuck on meditation practice (inside), on the conventional way of living that causes suffering (outside), or even on enlightenment (in between).

In practical terms, these distinctions can be quite useful. It is so helpful to bring mindfulness to our insides, to our emotional and cognitive tendencies. This is a central teaching in the Dhammapada, whose first line is "We are shaped by our mind." For example, when a coworker has left something poorly done, the mind is likely to begin to generate thoughts about that person's ineptitude or laziness. Mindfulness practice gives our consciousness the ability to turn inward and see those thoughts arising, to feel the alterations in our body: the tightening, the tensing, the suffering. By seeing these things without judging, we can let them be free to go, and then we are free to go, with a little more lightness and a little less likelihood of being unkind to ourselves and those around us. We train the mind to see what is arising in the mind. We notice our mental tendencies so we can be free from them.

Here's an odd thing: if we turn to look inside and focus on seeing thoughts and emotions rather than being caught by them and believing the stories they tell us, those very things that we thought were us, our self, or our "inside" become objects of our consciousness, things that we observe. They are now "outside."

Outside of what? And what were they originally inside? This is the puzzling kind of question that arises as we "turn around the light to shine within," as Shitou instructs later in this poem. Mahayana Buddhism tends to emphasize that any knowing of the answer to these kinds of puzzles is not correct, that the source of suffering is falsely believing our divisive conceptions, that we are enslaved in a cage of separateness created by conceptions. The Mahayana Middle Way is the way in between all opposites, all oppositions.

Let's go back to that coworker with the poorly done work. Where is our suffering when we are completely not-separate from the coworker, when the feelings and thoughts that arise are not just individual things, when they are part of an incomprehensibly and infinitely vast mutually operating interdependence?

One of the main themes of Vasubandhu's "Thirty Verses" is that our consciousness is all that we have to practice with; this is one of the reasons it's known as Consciousness-Only Buddhism. The other theme of the "Thirty Verses" is that everything is empty of a separate, continuing self—including consciousness. So it may be empty of a separate, lasting self, but in this moment we can practice because something appears to be here. Whatever is here right now is what we've got to work with, and we'll call it "mere consciousness." This is where we practice; this is where we can do our mindfulness, where we can realize unity, where we can give someone a hug, where we can get really angry, where we can forgive, where we can learn what happens to an old computer when we throw it "away," where we can have a warm cup of tea. Everything we usually call "inside" and "outside" is also empty, and any conception we put on these is actually just a convenient illusion that should be held very lightly. If we get stuck on "inside," we may forget that all the beauty and aggravation in our consciousness is just part of a vast, unknowable unfolding. If we get stuck on "outside," we chase after an ever-receding horizon of desires. If we get stuck on "inbetween," we may realize our total connection to everything in the universe but forget to pick the kids up from school. And so Vasubandhu gives us means to play with, practice, and understand "not stuck to inside, outside, or in between," and Shitou points to Vasubandhu's broad vision of practice in one line of verse.

But really, I'm a fool, sitting at a desk with rain falling gently on the other side of the open window, and Shitou is just calling attention to the fact that when he gets inside his little grass house he can barely claim that he's inside because the roof is full of holes where the light pours in. When he goes outside how can he say he's outside when the clouds and sky are always making a vast roof? And really, who can make a claim that he is walking some wonderful Middle Way, not stuck on "in between"? He's soft asleep in the afternoon while the ants check to see if he's washed his bowl.

## ETHICS AND MEDITATION

Having heard me talk about Shitou's work many times, my friend Martin has teased me that I'd end up writing twenty pages on the first word of this old poem. Perhaps I am overly verbose, but I like to think that I am just joyfully engaging in the incredible density of meaning and allusion that is to be found in such a little gem. Which is to say, I'd like to talk a bit more about "not stuck to inside, outside" from a different angle.

One could say that the Eightfold Path, the first and most central set of practices that define Buddhism, has an inside and an outside. Right effort, right mindfulness, and right concentration are inside, having to do with training the mind. Right speech, right action, and right livelihood are outside, having to do with how we engage in the world. When we teach Zen to beginners at our center, we put a lot of emphasis on meditation, because some sense of ethical behavior (the "outside" elements of the Eightfold Path) is usually already part of their upbringing and life, whereas meditation is not. Once people internalize and connect with a meditation practice, my hope is that they'll see that most of our teachings are about how to integrate ethical action and meditation, how to not be stuck on the inside or outside but instead freely flow.

When I first started meditating, it seemed pretty foreign. Sitting still and seeing how much stuff came floating up, in or out of the mind; tasting the moments of what felt like stillness but included so many vivid sounds of cars and birds and breathing, the play of light and shadow on a wall, the dull aches roving around in my back. My mind started to function in a different way when I sat zazen. It seemed wider, more open. It's hard to describe the sense of quiet, but I remember one hot June retreat where I was seated next to an open window. The Minnesota Zen Meditation Center is set on the edge of one of Minneapolis's many lakes, and this one attracts lots of summer celebrants. Several days into a retreat and into the deepening stillness, someone drove by with their car stereo blaring Bon Jovi's hair-metal anthem "You Give Love a Bad Name." Somehow the roar of the stereo and my huge silent laughter all seemed completely still. The vast "inside" of big mind is apparently even big enough for Bon Jovi.

The funny thing is that I'd get up from the cushion and about fifteen minutes later I'd be completely absorbed in the same kind of repetitive thinking I'd been doing my whole life. Then I was asked to be the guy who rings the bells, the timekeeper. This changed everything. First off, what if I failed? What if I lost track of time and left everyone sitting for an hour or perhaps hit the bell so hard someone had a heart attack? Secondly, was I not a grand fellow? Ringing bells and taking care of the essential activity of the Buddha Way? But sitting zazen with a job was the practice I was given, and after a while my mind once again became wider, more open. The obsessive self-centeredness started to fade and I became able to really devote myself to the task at hand. This has been one of the greatest things about practice for me—someone keeps asking me to do something new as part of the practice and I get to see all my patterned tendencies to shame, fear, grandiosity, control, attachment, and on and on, arise, and I get to stay with them as Zen practice. I get to let the mind shed all the thoughts and all the emotions and I get to grow, as the inside-oriented practice of meditation connects to outside activities. There are countless ways that practicing meditation with a community of other people is great, but this is one: you can be called on to draw your meditation off the cushion and into a wider and wider field.

When my teacher Tim Burkett offers a formal Zen initiation process, initiates study and vow to follow the ten precepts, the traditional guides for practicing the "outside" elements of the Eightfold Path: right speech, right action, and right livelihood. In the process of studying them, Tim has the students investigate personally and in groups both how following the precepts will help them promote well-being in the world and also how getting stuck to the precepts and following them rigidly could be harmful. For instance, the students explore how following the precept to not take what is not given could help alleviate suffering but also how sticking to that precept strictly might get in the way of helping people. He encourages them to view their vows with a big, open mind, a mind that looks inside and out. In his weekly talks and during retreats he tells stories about people who are really of service in the world, and he embodies service, both as a Zen teacher and the leader of a nonprofit that supports people with chronic mental illness. Almost every talk he gives encourages people to learn to draw the open, compassionate mind of meditation into a wider and wider field of activity in their daily lives.

If we stick to the inside practice, if our meditation just lives when we are sitting, it is very small. If we stick to outside practice, if our ethics are just about following some rules or ideas, they are narrow and they can cut us off from others who have a different rule book. But these can flow and live together; they can have their individual places and their mutuality. Where is the boundary between the water of the river and the water of the ocean, and wasn't it all once a part of the sky? When the self-centered tendencies of the mind settle down in meditation, we see connection and we let go of control. In zazen we offer what we are to the moment—in our daily lives can we offer what we are to the world? There is so much suffering there's no need for me to catalog it for you; just look in your heart, read the news, or listen to your family.

In his *Universal Recommendation for Zazen*, Dogen says, "You are taking care of the essential activity of the Buddha Way." This is an encouragement for our meditation practice, but it also has a much greater meaning. The Buddha Way is that which excludes nothing. Our practice is the essential activity of the Buddha Way, because our practice is whatever we are doing, because the world is the essential activity of the Buddha Way, and you are the essential activity of the Buddha Way. On the cushion or on the street, looking inside or looking out, here, the Buddha Way is where we are. May we take care of it.

# 7

## Retreat and Living in the World

PLACES WORLDLY PEOPLE LIVE,
HE DOESN'T LIVE.

Like modern-day America, Shitou's China was a place where people worked hard in an arena of competition to advance their condition, to gain wealth and prestige. Humans have been doing this for a long time, and a few people have chosen to walk away from it for just as long, seeing it as totally ineffective at promoting their welfare and the welfare of those around them. Buddha left his position as a prince, where he may perhaps have led with great benevolence, to a life of chosen poverty, humility, and service. Though it is rarely mentioned in those old texts, his path of abdication was also a life of bliss: a life of stillness when the sun blazed, of walking in the cool of the morning, of completely being in the great roar of the monsoon.

Most of the great exemplars of this tradition have outwardly manifested this renunciation of worldliness by living away from the great mass of people. Buddha walked all over northern India, staying in various groves and parklands and entering villages only to beg for food and to teach. Shitou and countless other monks often made their homes alone in the green of the mountains. Many followers of Chinese Zen lived in communal farming monasteries; rather than beg for food, these monks farmed as practice, doing the work that sustains life while withdrawing from the competitive self-seeking day-to-day world. However, these monasteries could easily become competitive little worlds of their own. Both experience and study leave me no doubt that our dear monks carried their conventional tendencies into their monasteries with them, just as we bring all our habits of mind and body into our meditation and our practice of being kind. By taking the body to the monastery or putting the mind into the light of meditation, though, we at least have the *possibility* of letting go.

About two hundred years ago, a Zen monk named Ryokan left behind the worldly politics of Japanese monastery life to live in a ramshackle hut near his hometown, begging for his food in an era when that ancient Buddhist practice had long since been left behind as a regular part of Japanese culture. He was, according to friends, beloved and considered pretty eccentric. He sometimes suffered a great deal from want of food, from cold weather, and from loneliness. He also left a record of his enormous love for the people he encountered, for the moon and the flowers, for the Buddha

Way, for walking, for simply being, in poetry and calligraphy that was admired by friends in his neighborhood. Long after his death many more people have come to appreciate his work. He is now one of the most widely read Japanese poets in the world, an amazingly beloved and influential figure.

It's fairly easy to see how Ryokan's dedication to not living where worldly people live has been a benefit to the world. Countless people every day draw inspiration to be kind, patient, humble, and open-minded from the poetry he produced in his renunciation, but I think it's harder to see how withdrawing from worldly life in this way is of benefit when we think of the thousands or perhaps millions of people who've done it and weren't also incredibly gifted poets. We should remember that there could be no Ryokan if those others hadn't shown the Way, hadn't first withdrawn. It is hard to see that our practice of retreating from worldly things; of letting go of thoughts, ideas, and views; of being still; of just resting in what is, on a cushion in a quiet corner, is a gift to the world, a gift to everyone we know and everyone we don't. There is so much suffering, competition, and conflict in the world, just to be at peace for a little while is an incredible offering.

Shitou says the person in this hut does not live where worldly people live. I'm guessing almost everyone reading this book *does* live where worldly people live. Working a job, perhaps raising a family, certainly part of some kind of net of social connection—but we can step away from worldly things in meditation practice, and in retreat. My teacher Tim is always encouraging this: "Do retreats, spend time steeping yourself in silence." We offer half- to seven-day retreats every month, during which we quietly work together to sustain each other. We cook, clean, walk, and stay still without talking and interacting, so that we can let go of our worldly worries and be in our moments with a fresh, relaxed, and open mind. And when we go back to our families and our jobs and all our cares, we bring a little lightness.

Tim's other job involves petitioning legislators for funding for housing and care for the seriously mentally ill. All those legislators with their own agendas, plenty of egos presumably, countless other people competing for attention and interest, for time and money for their causes, and what is the Zen way? For my teacher, it seems to me, the way is to be there, to be in the world of worldly affairs, offering himself in the service of others. And how does this agree with Shitou's vision? Because the present moment is not a place of worldly concerns if we are *really there*. Wherever we are with presence of mind we can let go of or be free from worldly matters: pride, desire, anger, the need to control others. I've heard Tim talk of seeing himself judging a politician with a Bible on his desk who wants to cut funding for the mentally ill, feeling the anger, feeling that powerful sense of separation when we think we're right and the other is wrong. I've heard him talk of taking up his practice of being present and available, seeing his complete connection, his interdependence, with the man across the desk, and returning completely to the activity of asking for support for the suffering—and accepting that it may not be given, and opening his heart.

# 8

## What Do You Mean When You Say "Love"?

"Love" is a great big word. Like the time machine in the television show *Doctor Who*, it's bigger on the inside. That time machine looks like a simple phone booth from outside, but inside it's vast beyond the limits of exploration. "Love": So small, just four letters on which we hang our greatest literature, our greatest sufferings, our families, those moments when our greatest human capacities are realized. Clearly we're not talking about the same thing when we say "I love blueberry pie," "I love my mother," "I love Brad Pitt," or "I love yoga," and surely when we say "I love my son" the dented exterior of the word barely shows the vastness of what that means.

Shitou does not mention in the poem anything that he loves, only saying what he doesn't love: "realms worldly people love." This is actually pretty common for Buddhist teachers; in one old sutra Buddha gives a talk about love that is fairly long but is reasonably paraphrased thusly: "He who loves fifty people has fifty woes; he who loves no one has no woes." Frankly, although I know the first part to be true, I don't know about the last half. I do not believe I know anyone who doesn't love anyone, I certainly don't know anyone who doesn't have any woes. So what is Buddha, with all his insight, up to here? When he says "love," he means attachment, wanting, desire, having an idea of how things should be and being stuck on it. Most of the time, part of loving someone involves this attachment. When I don't see my son for a while, I tend to feel sad and cranky. When my friend is absorbed in his own problems and goes on and on without seeming to really hear or see me, I feel angry and want to walk away. During the process of my father's death I experienced a huge range of suffering. I didn't want to lose him.

So insofar as love is attachment, it is intimately connected to suffering—like we are. However, I think it's worth trying to establish a definition of love that we can use in a positive light and that won't put us in opposition to the great admirable mass of Buddhist literature. Why? Because I think the word "love" can be inspiring. Not always, of course; when you say you love blueberry pie, you're not talking about a love that wants nothing but to be of service to the blueberry pie with no interest or expectation of any return or results, of course. But sometimes when we use the word, we mean we're willing to give our whole effort without any attachment. Sometimes when our baby is crying, we do everything we can to try and help the baby be at ease, and sometimes we're so absorbed in this activity that we don't wait for or expect the baby to change and instead just give ourselves to the activity. Sure, other times we're frustrated and annoyed that the crying doesn't stop, we feel ashamed that something is wrong with us as parents, and we don't know how to help our baby just be okay. Nonattached love and attachment are often very tightly interwoven in who we are—this is to be human.

In Dylan Thomas's "Do Not Go Gentle into that Good Night," he urges a dying parent to "Rage, rage, against the dying of the light." When a loved one is dying and we find ourselves carrying one who carried us, when we find ourselves in fluorescent, tiled, and sterile buildings waiting and not knowing what to do, we may rage, we may despair, we will taste the brutal pangs of attachment that drove Buddha from his palace and into years of practice and then profound peace. But it is quite common for there to be some moments where our love is still, where we are not wishing that Mom were well or that death would never come, and we are merely there, we are merely here, offering our attention. Actually, not even offering our attention, because this love does not see someone other than ourselves, outside of ourselves, to offer anything to; it just completely manifests, in the form of everything completed and connected by the hospital bedside in the dying light of day and the birth of night. There is only love.

The ability of a love bound by lots of attachment to expand into a love that is purely letting go is easiest for me to find in these extremities of the human condition, but it is manifested throughout Zen practice and it is arguably the purpose of Zen practice. Suzuki Roshi said, "Zen is *making your best effort* in each *moment forever*." Is that not love that's letting go? Without wanting results or having expectations, without attachment? Sure, this love sounds impossible, but like my teacher Tim says, "It's not impossible, it's inconceivable." Dive in!

When we sit in meditation, we let the mind that picks and chooses have a little rest; we see the realms our little worldly personages love, and we let them go. In our lives we can get all wound up and bound in thoughts and feel like our practice is pointless; other times we might get hungry and try and practice really hard to get enlightenment. Hopefully, then we go see our teacher, and we just come back to letting the mind rest. Soon the mind starts to be at rest on its own— soon the picking and choosing comes to a halt, and our minds open up. The attachment-manufacturing plant closes for the weekend, and the workers get to stroll home in their greasy coveralls and give great big hugs to their kids without thinking about whether their kids are good enough at math or have the right friends. We just come home to what is and are there for it; we see that what is here is only love.

# 9

## Everything's Included

Autonomy and interdependence, alienation and connection—these are the key matters of "Though the hut is small, it includes the entire world." They are also the central themes in Hua Yen Buddhism, a school of thought and practice that arose in China fairly contemporaneously with Zen during the latter half of the first millennium CE. The emphasis of this school was the interpenetration, or interdependence, of all phenomena. The idea that all things are infinitely interconnected has been a part of pretty much every type of Buddhism, but the Hua Yen school really made it the central pillar of understanding. In simplest terms, realizing our connection—rather than our separation—can be profoundly healing. Aren't the most painful times with your loved ones the ones where you feel most separate?

However, separateness is not the only pitfall here; we can get lost in interdependence. We can lose our sense of personal authority, autonomy, and responsibility. We need to realize that we're both interdependent and autonomous, both together and apart.

Hua Yen describes the world as being a fourfold realm, and the Chinese characters for these realms are the same ones Shitou uses, translated here as "the entire world." The teaching of the fourfold realm is quite complex, but in practical terms it can be boiled down to the fact that each thing is intimately connected to every other thing, each thing is an expression of the interdependence of everything else, the whole universe is an expression of each individual thing, and each thing is exactly itself. In other words: everything is interdependent; you are just the universe expressing itself; your actions have infinite impact; and each thing is simply itself, you are you.

I'm reminded of a story my teacher Tim told of his teacher Suzuki Roshi. Suzuki had been talking a great deal about how things were not separate, were the same rather than different. A student wasn't buying it and asked, "You're always talking about how everything's the same, but what's the point? You're five feet tall, I'm over six feet; you're teaching, I'm listening—how can you say we're the same?" Suzuki responded, "You're stuck on difference; if you were stuck on everything being the same, I'd teach about how everything is different." Shitou shows us we don't have to be stuck on either one; the one in the hermitage realizes his connection to all things, and he realizes that he's right in his spot, with the details of life to take careful care of.

We are the same, and we are different. The grass hut is small, and it includes the entire world. You are you, and you have all your personal tendencies and desires; you have your choice in each moment, and you are the way the universe is manifesting itself right now.

Each moment we have a choice, an opportunity. We can do something helpful, we can doing something harmful, we can be completely unaware and operate out of habit. We have this chance to use each moment of choice that we are given to take care of our lives and the world around us. Let's take this chance together. It is a beautiful way to live.

On the other hand, since we are merely an expression of the interdependence of everything, we can't even begin to know all the things that lead us to make the choices we make. You can't choose all the infinite things that led to you being here in this moment as you are; you can't choose your vast array of unconscious motivations that cause your choices. If we only consider the impact of our parents' and our grandparents' behavior on our unconscious tendencies, even this is beyond comprehension and is still not even one trillionth of a trillionth of all the things we could list that come together to make us what we are right now.

A recent experiment showed that people were more generous if they had recently held a cup with a warm beverage in it than if they had held a cold one. Obviously this was not something the participants were consciously aware of. How did this come to be a tendency that humans have? How many other similar tendencies will we never know about? And yet we act and think like we know what's going on all the time; we get stuck on our little views of our self. We have a self that can make a choice, and there is just the universe making itself in a form we think is our self, with a choice we think is our own, but which is just the universe expressing itself. Knowing that we have a choice helps us take full responsibility for our actions. Knowing that we are unconsciously expressing infinite conditioning opens up room for compassion for ourselves and others, in all our countless failures, suffering, and harmful acts.

In his *Genjokoan*, Dogen Zenji says, "To study the Way is to study the self; to study the self is to forget the self." If we take care of our grass hut, if we take care of what is here, of our little place in the world, with wholehearted attention and curiosity, we can forget our separateness and realize our connection, realize that our hut contains the entire world. This is the promise of Zen. We can offer what we are to what is, but we are not even making an offering, because "what is" is already what we are, and it's just doing what it does. We say this is realizing the Way, but the Way is always realizing itself; the world is always realizing itself, and we are always realizing the world. This is why we practice.

# 10

## Ten Feet Square

IN TEN FEET SQUARE, AN OLD MAN ILLUMINES
FORMS AND THEIR NATURE.

You don't need very much to see deeply into things.

The promise of the Buddhist tradition is that if you devote yourself to simplicity and quiet, if you let the mind settle down, profound and liberating insights appear. Instead of trying to investigate an encyclopedic array of things to gain knowledge, our monk is just looking at what is right there with him in his ten-foot-square home. In the Vimalakirti Sutra, the eponymous Mahayana layman hosts Manjushri, the bodhisattva of wisdom, for a discussion of Dharma in his ten-by-ten room, which then miraculously accommodates a vast multitude of aspirants, buddhas, and bodhisattvas.

Countless others have retreated to small and simple cells to live and practice, to touch something vast and deep. Taking care of what is immediately around us, our ten feet square, there is plenty of room to illumine forms and their nature, to see things in their immediate uniqueness and to see their unknowable interdependence, to see a dandelion just bursting into bloom, and at that same time see the wind, water, and sun that brought it here from a seed.

Dogen teaches, "Here is the place, here the Way unfolds." It doesn't matter where the here is; what matters is that we take the opportunity to practice where we are. We have a vast proliferation of media, information, and technology these days. It's easy to communicate with people all over the world instantaneously, to hear what's going on in countless other lives, to fly across the globe. The capacity to connect with and learn from people from different cultures and backgrounds and with widely varying views seems like it should be a good thing, and surely it can be. However, it's not clear that all this news, these electronic social networks, and this travel are actually helping people feel more deeply connected to their fellow humans. What really matters—if we want to realize the depth of our interdependence—is the quality of our mind.

Buddhist literature teaches consistently that training the mind to focus and be still is necessary to deepen our sense of peace and harmony with all things. This training requires putting some gentle limits on the mind's tendency to dart from one thing to another, from one worry to one desire, to one thought you've repeated a thousand times, from one page to another on the computer's screen. This is why it helps to find ten feet square where you can concentrate your practice. You can sit down on a meditation cushion or a park bench, set your feet on a yoga mat, spend a few days at a retreat center, or just turn the gaze down wherever you are— and bring your mind to the breath and body. When we draw the gaze inward we actually have a chance to see through our habits of body and mind and see what is here right now in our little corner of the world, which is always vast and amazing.

Ten feet square is not a lot of room. I don't know if Shitou ever wished he'd built a bigger hut, but I can tell you that there have been plenty of times when staying on my cushion seemed really tough. Someone came to me during a retreat I was leading a while back and said, "Meditation was going great until the sun came out, and now I'm just thinking about riding my motorcycle and working in my yard." The practice of limiting our range so the mind can quiet down and focus puts us right up close to the mind's tendency to think there's something better somewhere else. Although there are a lot of teachings about the profound peace, stillness, and insight found in meditation in the early Buddhist literature, the Dhammapada also gives us this: "Just as a fish hooked and left on the sand thrashes about in agony, the mind being trained in meditation trembles all over."

If we stay put through whatever comes up in mind, if we stay true to our ten feet square, if we stay com-mitted to being right where we are, then the greatest possibility for freedom arises: the opportunity to be free from our limited views and habits by shining a little light on things as they are, in both their autonomy and their interconnection, their form and their nature. Instead of flitting from one idea to the next, from one place to another, from one more cursory online connection, or to one more piece of sensational news, we can settle down in this place, wherever it is—this activity, whatever it is—and shine the light of our hearts and minds on whatever connection we are a part of right now.

# 11

## Trust, Faith, and Ease

A GREAT VEHICLE BODHISATTVA TRUSTS
WITHOUT DOUBT.

The trust, the faith, that is held up in this line, that is promised throughout the Buddhist tradition, is not trust in any truth, idea, or ideology. We might say that this is trust in things-as-they-are, and that's pretty good but isn't exactly right, because it's a trust that includes and goes beyond anything we can experience or understand. Trust here is about a condition of consciousness that is completely at ease. It is about the absence of anxiety; it is about being at rest.

"Great vehicle" is the literal translation of Mahayana, the great vehicle to carry all beings to liberation from suffering; a bodhisattva is the ferryman or woman who devotes him- or herself to helping people on the voyage. A Great Vehicle bodhisattva is a deity, a supernatural embodiment of Buddhism's highest ideals; it is the old man who in the last line illumined forms and their nature, the person in the hut living here calmly; it is you if your heart is devoted to the way of liberation from suffering. These lofty ideas, of a Great Vehicle, of deities, of universal liberation, are here to help us see our connection to the greatest possibilities of the human heart, because trust in the unknowable, ever-changing nature of things is scary.

To experience fear and anxiety is a human tendency. There are good reasons to feel fear. When I ride my bike and a car nearly hits me, the jolt of fear helps me to immediately, instinctively get out of the way. In general, though, we experience an enormous amount of totally unhelpful anxiety. The amount of time I've spent worrying about being late to things is astounding. We all have our own areas of specialization: fear about money; fear about children, parents, lovers, or jobs. These can all certainly be helpful. If you are afraid because your lover tends to insult you, maybe it's time to leave; if you don't have enough money to have food, shelter, and medicine, it's time to take action, to seek help. However, my experience is that the amount of time, energy, and mental activity devoted to fears is absurdly out of proportion.

The true test of the value of things is whether they promote wellness for all; I encourage you to observe the fear and anxiety in your mind and body and see whether they help you and others. If not, there's no need to judge or throw out these feelings, just recognize them for what they are. This is actually the beginning of the bodhisattva's trust—to have enough confidence to turn the light inward and look at the fear itself, rather than the shadow it is casting that we think is reality. A friend was recently telling me about a colleague he was worried was angry with him; later my friend found out that the colleague had been completely unaware that any hard feelings or judgments had come up. My friend got a chance to see in stark relief how anxiety creates a world that is not there.

The bodhisattva's trust includes the knowledge that all things that come into being will pass away; it includes the knowledge that suffering is an inherent aspect of existence; it includes the knowledge that the true nature of things is completely outside of and always within everything we think or perceive; it includes completely not knowing what is going to happen, what has happened, and what is happening right now. There is a human tendency to try and feel safe by categorizing, organizing, and shrinking consciousness into something we think we can manage—and then to worry about this shrunken, limited view of things, which actually makes us feel unsafe. But it doesn't have to be that way. It is possible to let go into not-knowing and let all the things we like and don't like appear and disappear. This is what we practice in meditation, and it is a way of being that we can bring to the world.

So Zen does not offer you trust that you will have a heavenly cloud to go to after death, and it should not give you a feeling of righteousness in having the truth laid out in some teachings given long ago. Instead, it gives you the opportunity to do a practice of trusting what is, which can open your heart to trusting the nature of things in their complete unknowability. This trust then just manifests itself naturally and kindly.

When you're in a meeting and everyone takes sides and the debate's pitch rises, you can offer your voice clearly and assertively but with trust, without being caught by the fear that your side won't prevail, because no one is on any other side from you. When your child is making choices that seem so clearly to be harmful, you can show you care, help guide him or her, trust, and let go, knowing that your life, your child's life, and all the lives that have ever been lived are all connected in ways far, far beyond anything that knowledge can ever touch. Thus, without a doubt, you can live the bodhisattva's trust and vast compassion.

# 12

## Don't Judge

This type of language—"the middling or lowly"—is used throughout Zen literature to refer to people's intellectual capacities: refined or common, sharp or dull. I don't think it's helpful, and I don't think we should emulate it. I love Shitou, I love this poem, and I love this tradition, but I don't think it helps people to point out that they are lowly or dull. I understand that it is useful to recognize that people have different capacities, but there are ways to talk about it that are harmful and ways that are not.

In an early sutra, Buddha gives an extremely simple teaching to a visiting student; the Buddha just sits silently with him, and the student experiences awakening. Buddha's attendant, Ananda, is impressed with the student's readiness, and Buddha explains, "A good horse runs even at the shadow of the whip." He goes on to say that there are different types of people just as there are different types of horses. The second-best horse runs just before the whip hits the skin, the poor horse runs when it feels the pain on its skin, and the lowliest runs when it feels the pain of the whip down in its bones. In this case, Buddha is not talking about intellectual capacity but about the readiness with which someone realizes liberation from suffering. He's talking about how much suffering one has to experience before one begins to work for, or realize, liberation. Still, I'm not aware of any old stories in which Buddha actually tells someone they are a poor or lowly horse; in sutra after sutra he meets people and offers them his presence and wisdom, whether they are kings, monks, farmers, a naked and crazed woman on the bank of a river, or the most reviled and feared murderer in the land.

I'd like to do away with the idea that any horse is better than any other. They all just want to have pasture, room to roam, some tasty grass, maybe a carrot for a treat; if one won't run, we can enjoy watching it walk.

In the *Universal Recommendation for Zazen*, Dogen says, "Make no distinction between the dull and sharp-witted; if you concentrate your effort single-mindedly, that in itself is wholeheartedly engaging the Way." His statement is a response to the prevalence of this kind of language in Zen, and his view is that participating in this moment with our whole hearts is the Way, regardless of our capacities.

When I teach a group of long-term Zen practitioners, I may use all kinds of technical Buddhist terms, or I may make seemingly contradictory statements that point to freedom of mind, to the unknowability of everything. When I meet a cashier at the grocery store, I smile. When I'm with my teenage son, I try to listen. When I'm teaching meditation to newcomers, I talk about breathing. I do all these things with varying degrees of success, but I try not to think of one as better than another, and I often don't, because my Zen training allows me not to.

Sometimes I teach meditation to people in jail, chemical dependency treatment, or mental health facilities. This is quite wonderful, in part because when I was much younger, before I quit drinking and using drugs, I spent time as a prisoner and patient in places like that, and those experiences make me love the people there all the more. But it is wonderful in even greater part because they are simply people who want to be well. Everyone suffers—but the people in these kinds of facilities are very close to this First Noble Truth, and it makes me feel close to them. Sometimes, though, I feel uncomfortable or frustrated working in these places; the intensity of the suffering can be pervasive, the people there not receptive to instruction, uninterested in any kind of connection.

When I experience this, my practice is to turn inward and see what I'm feeling and thinking—and to let go of thoughts about how the students are not ready for the teaching or are poor horses. To see how

I'm judging them, comparing them to others; how I want to succeed, to be liked. I realize then that my frustration is not about the horse; it's about the whip. It's about me. I don't have any interest in being a whip. I'm interested in being a good friend. I'd like to stand end-to-end with my fellow horses munching grass, while we brush flies off each other's faces with our tails. So when I feel this kind of frustration while teaching, I can always come back to just being present to whoever I am with and offering my effort for our well-being.

The simplest expression of Buddha's instruction on right speech is "speak only what is true, and kind, and timely." He used the metaphor of the horse to make a point about teaching and about why some people can let go of suffering quicker than others. He said it in a way that was timely, to a person who wanted to hear it, not to someone who would feel judged or belittled. When you need to decide what classes you or your children should take, or when you are looking for a job, think and talk about capacity. But we can look out for terms like "lowly," "middling," "slow," "dumb," or "immature"—judgmental terms that we wouldn't want to hear used about us—and let them go. We can find a way to express what is helpful in a kind way.

So let me rephrase Shitou's line: "Us humans worry about things."

# 13

## Life and Death Is the Great Matter

It seems pretty clear that this hut will collapse, doesn't it? It's made of grass, it's not going to last forever, and anyway, why is this something we'd wonder about? It's not such a big deal, just a little hut. But Shitou is making another shift in the fluid views of identity presented in this poem.

This hut has become ourselves. He says people wonder whether the hut will perish or not because the hut is now a name for the self, for the place in which we live, for whatever we call ourselves. We construct the self, and we live in it; it's our abode.

The question of whether we live on or die after the body stops functioning runs throughout human culture. Christianity promises eternal life after the death of the body; many Buddhists believe that after death we are reborn in other forms; many secularists believe the self ends when the physical processes of life cease in the body. Lots of answers have been presented and believed, but the presence of so many answers makes it seems like a great big question to me.

Seeing the pain associated with death was one of the principal things that set the Buddha on the path to try and find a way beyond suffering, and it was not long after my father's death that I set foot on the Zen path, trying to deal with the pain. When death comes to someone close to us, we touch one of the most difficult and painful aspects of being human; the dissatisfaction that follows impermanence is in its most harsh and stark relief. I find it remarkable that Buddha, who was raised believing people were reincarnated after death, found death to be painful, and that many monotheists, who are taught that after death they will go to an eternal blissful heaven and be reunited with their loved ones, still find death so painful. It's as though no matter how strong or consoling your beliefs, still some part of you cannot be assuaged in the face of this reality. As someone who was raised humanist with the belief that death is a final and irrevocable end to the self, I've often wondered whether dealing with death would be easier with the idea of an eternal hereafter, but from observing people I really don't know.

Shitou doesn't seem to know whether or not things die. This is a question he doesn't answer. He doesn't even ask it, only saying that the "middling or lowly" might be worried about the fate of his hut. Which is odd; it seems pretty clear that we die, right? There are a lot of ideas about what happens after death, but what kind of person would claim that there is no death? As someone who stood in the room while my dear father's body went from warm to cold, I can tell you it seemed very clear that death had occurred. But I'll tell you something else: as I walk around on the face of this earth, saying things just like my father used to say, in a voice very like his, seeing thoughts and views that my father held appear in my mind, it is not so clear to me that death has occurred.

My teacher Tim sometimes talks about his teacher Suzuki Roshi visiting him in dreams. Some people might say that a dream is the result of the mind processing memories and creating visions while we sleep, so these dreams are constructed by Tim's unconscious. Other people might say that Roshi's spirit is alive and is visiting his student to encourage him. These are ideas. In one view Suzuki is dead and only his memory continues in Tim's mind; in the other Suzuki lives. Both views are dependent on the idea that there is a Suzuki that lived or lives and died or didn't, that there was a person in the hut, a Suzuki living in a shell, a body, an identity that came to be and passed away.

In *Genjokoan*, Dogen tells us that we may think we aren't enlightened, but we are. How encouraging! He says, "When you first seek Dharma you imagine that you are far away from its environs, but Dharma is already correctly transmitted; you are immediately your original self." He then explains that this is true because we are impermanent, that though we may think we are a continuous being looking out (of our hut, perhaps) at a changing world, there is no fixed being resting in any abode; there is only change. He then points out that since we are just change, rather than a fixed thing, we can't die, because we were never born in the first place. We are not things separate from anything, things with brief, impermanent lives; there is only an unknowable, infinite, interdependent process of transience, of the universe realizing itself. Or, we might say, there is only realization, enlightenment.

To sum up: you're enlightened, because you don't exist, so you don't have to worry about dying, because you were never born. This all sounds very heady, but he gives a very simple instruction in the midst of it all: "Practice intimately and return to where you are." This is the means by which we can see that nothing at all has an unchanging self, how we can see we are just an aspect of infinite transformation. This is the path to seeing beyond birth and death.

When we practice this way and see change, when there is some loosening of our view that some things persist, there is some opening. I don't hope for Buddhism to take away the pain of death. I do know that, having practiced all these years, I'm a whole lot more at ease when big changes come. When my consciousness seems to be a continuation of my father's, I can be curious; when I miss him, I can be close to that feeling; and when I have a dream where he comes to see me, I can embrace him.

# 14

## Who Is the Original Master?

The original master is present. Who is this person, this original master? Zen Buddhists claim Buddha as their original master, the founder of their lineage; Shitou is saying he's here. Are you present? Are you here? Is there something else you can be?

"Buddha" is a term that is used in many ways. Sometimes it refers to the historical figure who founded Buddhism, Siddhartha Gotama; sometimes it refers to what is also called the *dharmakaya*: the unconceived, timeless, and infinite, what Thich Nhat Hanh calls "interbeing," beyond interconnection; it is the complete interpenetration of all phenomena. When he had his great realization, Siddhartha saw through the conceptions that caused him to feel separate from the rest of the universe; that's why he stopped chasing after personal pleasure and went beyond suffering, and that's why he devoted the rest of his life to serving his community. What made Buddha "Buddha" was seeing through separateness. So though in one sense he was a man who lived a long time ago and who used to go into a village to humbly beg for food, in another he is everywhere at all times, because the reason he is Buddha is that he is not separate from anything. This is also why you are Buddha.

When we say "not separate," when we discuss dharmakaya, the original master, we're pointing toward something that is impossible to put into words. The Chinese character that is translated here as "master" also means "host." The host is present. There are many complex and subtle Zen teachings based on the idea of host and guest; in simple terms we can say the host is the same as the dharmakaya—beyond conception, excluding nothing. Guests, on the other hand, are anything viewed as separate from anything else. When we think of the host, it is a guest, because we are thinking of it as something separate, but the thought is still the host because the host is not separate from anything. Ideas are guests, thoughts are guests—we should be cordial to them, but we don't need to base our whole lives around what they tell us. Guests appear to come and go, huts are built and seem to perish, but the host, the original master, is beyond time.

The original master is present; the host is present. Right here in this moment we call experience. I am running my fingers across a silver keyboard in the early morning light; you are reading text; in this moment the host is present. The I, the you, the keyboard, and the text are all guests that we know are present, but the host is here as well. Wherever you turn, the original master is here; Buddha's enlightenment is just this beyond-separateness. It is not outside of, or separate from, the guests. In every moment Buddha is present, whether looking out through your eyes, ringing as the sound of a distant ambulance, or falling from the sky and soaking down into the earth.

# 15

## Have You Ever Transcended Space and Time?

NOT DWELLING SOUTH OR NORTH, EAST OR WEST.

In the movie *I Heart Huckabees* an "existential detective" asks her new client, "Have you ever transcended space and time?" The client, bewildered, answers, "Yes. No. Uh, time, not space. No, I don't know what you're talking about." From a Zen perspective, all his answers are good, none of them are true, and the last one is likely the best. All of them show a mind being freed by having its limits, its basic ideas, tested. Transcending space and time sounds pretty exciting, pretty "out there," but is actually utter simplicity; you're already doing it. Talking about it unfortunately is complicated. Sometimes it's not helpful to create complicated words for simple things, but because this simple thing is so hard to realize, so vast and so freeing, it has come up many times in Buddhism, under many names. I'm using the term "transcend," but I might as accurately say "see through" space and time, or "realize the emptiness" of space and time, or maybe just "forget about" space and time.

"The original master is present" means you are present and Buddha is present. "Not dwelling south or north, east or west" means that though we are present, we're not in a location.

You're probably experiencing a range of visual images, thoughts, sounds, and other sensory things right now. Our consciousness is habituated through evolution, culture, and personal habit to categorize this data, to construct a finite world. We can do this very, very rapidly, so fast we're unaware we're doing it. The sense that there is an "I" perceiving objects is almost always there, for instance, as is the sense that some things are nearer and others farther away, that certain things are the body that is attached to "I" and certain things are not that body, that we are located in the middle of some things that we perceive are changing, that time is passing. You know that you are in a particular place, no question. A coffee shop? Your bedroom? An infant, on the other hand, doesn't know she's in a place that is different than other places; it's not clear that she even knows there is a place that's other than herself. For the rest of us, it's hard to see and hard to explain that these senses of categories and differences are not fundamentally true. To see it, we let the mind rest in meditation; to explain it, I'll use an old Buddhist way.

We can't have south without north. South and north are ideas we have for explaining the surface of the earth in relation to the sun and the earth's magnetic field, but the distinction between them only exists in our minds; the parts of the earth that we describe as "south" and "north" are operating completely dependently. South is not saying, "Hey, that's my air, North, you can't have it!" North does not reply, "Well, if you keep the air, South, I'm keeping all the water!" The water and the air are flowing freely always, and any line we draw must finally be arbitrary. Instead of thinking of south and north as two things, it's probably just as accurate to describe them as one thing: the relationship between south and north.

The north/south relationship is dependent on its relationship with our minds; our categorizing brains are the only things interested in the subject. Now, our minds are completely dependent on air and water, which is constantly moving through our bodies and our brains. So it's most accurate to say that "south" and "north" are a relationship between south, north, mind, water, and air.

We can continue this line of reasoning for as long as consciousness functions and never run out of things on which north and south depend, because they do not exist as real entities separate from anything else. In Buddhism we would say they are empty—empty of persisting, separate selves. We might also use the shorthand of saying they don't exist, or there is no north, no south. Here Shitou says, "not dwelling south or north, east or west."

We can make a similar argument about front and back, above and below, and before and after. This is the kind of approach the extraordinarily influential Mahayana teacher Nagarjuna made in the early part of the first millennium. Numerous times he takes a basic, central idea we have about the world—such as space, time, self, or motion—and uses a cognitive, logical argument to demonstrate that it is not a real thing, that it is empty of a separate, persisting self. This method points at something that we can realize through meditation practice and is already manifesting itself right now as us: the emptiness of every cognizable form; the interpenetration, or dependent co-arising, of all things. When we let the mind be still, when we give it a big, safe space to quiet down the habits that construct separation, the impulse to categorize fades away. We transcend our preconceptions.

Realizing how our most basic sense of reality is not showing us the truth is valuable because it is freeing. It releases us from the tendency to be bound by our fixed views. That these harm us is most obvious when we are in an entrenched argument. Just look at the Middle East; isn't it painful to hear, year after year, the same grievances, the same rage, the same despair, the same views, fixed along a boundary line? Can we see in this the reflection of our own old fixed familial conflicts and political rants?

Fixed views on the much more subtle level of tiny, day-to-day worries hold us back from just meeting each moment with ease. When you start to clench your jaw as a day's frustrations mount, you may find that you feel very tightly locked in one place by aggravations. You can remind yourself of the possibility of being free of the confines of your small mind, that cramped attic, of opening up to a big mind that is not bound by location or ideas about how things "should" be going, an unlocatable mind that meets with some surprise and wonder whatever comes.

It's good to have our ideas of south and north, to know where we are, but it's also good to have a mind that is so relaxed and free that it can go anywhere, be anywhere, and not be at all, without any worries.

# 16

## The Foundation of Freedom

FIRMLY BASED ON STEADINESS, IT CAN'T
BE SURPASSED.

### STEADY PRACTICE

Autumn is beginning in Minnesota where I live, and
the leaves are beginning to lose their deep green and
gain a soft yellow. The kids I love are getting older,
leaving behind kid things and finding adult ones. My
mom says that since her knees are going, this is the last
year she will be able to go on our annual family backpacking trip into the mountains. Weeds are growing all
over our grass hut, fresh weeds.

Today, I'm heading down to a rural retreat center,
where I'll be bathed in the evidence of the changes fall
brings: the cool, the colors, the birds heading south.
There, I will immerse myself in steady practice: moving
slowly, sitting still, living in a way that allows me to give
my whole attention to tying my shoes, cooking rice, and
having tea. This commitment to steadiness is the door-
way to the unsurpassable freedom the Dharma offers.

Sometimes Buddhists use words to stretch the bounds of consciousness, but more often we recommend the practice of simplicity.

Steadiness amid change is a common theme in Buddhist literature. Early teachings recommend training the mind to stay concentrated on the coming and going of things, their appearance and their passing away. Without this kind of training, the body and mind tend to be swept up in a reactive froth of emotion and thought. On the radio, we hear the voice of a politician we disagree with, and our body tenses; the mind starts to fire off a string of thoughts about his faults, the stupidity of his supporters, the disaster that will befall us if he is successful. Or we hear the politician we love, and we feel encouraged and supported, perhaps self-righteous and superior. This kind of reactivity doesn't just keep us from being at ease; it reduces our potential to help other people by trapping us in our self-centered views.

Shitou uses various terms for "calm" and "ease" numerous times in this poem, but here he says, "Firmly based on steadiness." The promise that this poem holds out for us is not realized by just relaxing, by just being at our ease, but takes a firm commitment to practice. And the main practice, the practice that supports all others, is sitting meditation.

The Chinese characters translated as "firmly based on steadiness" could also be roughly translated as "foundation site firm, strong." When we sit down to meditate we make a firm foundation. At my place of practice we encourage our meditators to find a way of sitting that is strongly rooted. In a chair we find the right height to support an upright posture; on a meditation cushion we make sure the knees are on the ground so the body is well balanced. A stable body is the foundation for stillness for practice. I recall sitting in Hokyoji Zen Practice Community's zendo while a storm raged outside, deeply hearing the roar of the rain on the roof and the crack of nearby thunder while the temperature inside fell, and all was completely still; twenty people sitting soft, strong, and steady together.

So far in this poem Shitou shows a monk at ease, relaxed amid change, attuned to the vastness, and taking care of the small things. Now he's brought us a reminder that the foundation of this life is meditation, a mind that's not swept away. His audience at the time he wrote was mostly monks who were very devoted to Buddhist practice, so he started with ease to remind them to not get stuck on the idea of struggling to realize the Way, of having the very firmest foundation of all. When practice gets intense and feels like a struggle, it's often good to recall the message of ease. But most of us today are not monks and might be taking our practice pretty easy already; if you do not have a firm and steady practice as a regular part of your life, and the message of this poem resonates with you, find

the practice, find support for the practice. The promise of this poem, of Buddhism, is not realized without
a commitment to meditation. We can stay here, right
now, on our foundation, and we can offer ourselves the
chance to find our place through meditation.

## UNSURPASSABLE

This monk who tells us about his simple life with nothing of value is now saying it's unsurpassable: something
awesome, something incomparable.

In Zen temples across the world for over a thousand
years, monks have devoted themselves to very simple
practices: wholeheartedly sweeping leaves from the
front steps; complete, loving attention to cutting car-
rots; silent, easeful, upright sitting. They wear humble,
patched robes in muted colors; they make countless
simple bows. They claim no grand and radiant deity,
and yet each morning while reciting the Heart Sutra
they chant that the Prajnaparamita Mantra is the
"great miraculous mantra, the great bright mantra, the
incomparable mantra, the supreme mantra." The mantra itself is just a few old words that point to letting
go of fixed ideas. But this recitation is a lesson in the
power and value of lofty language.

Politicians well know the power of this kind of language. Hope. Change. Strength. Forward. Huge ban-

ners and huge letters proclaim them. The words are big, the meanings are big, the feelings are big, and big feelings are motivating. I have been inspired to action, promoting peace and justice, by speeches that used this kind of grand language. Religions know the power of this kind of language too: "God is great," "I am the way, the light, and the love," "God created Heaven and Earth," "Gone, gone, gone beyond, gone completely beyond." These words bring tears to our eyes, they are powerful, they go to our hearts, and they don't usually spend a lot of time in our minds.

For this last reason, I have often been quite suspicious of them. I recall the wrenching scene in the movie *Saving Private Ryan* where a devout young sniper repeats a lofty scripture from the Bible while methodically shooting his enemies from a bell tower. This is a scene made real daily in the minarets of Syria, where snipers fire on their fellow men in the name of Allah. In Japan during World War II, Buddhist monks supported an expansionist war. People have raised the grand words of their religion while oppressing, judging, invading, and killing innumerable times.

I don't think we should run from the power of awesome language; I think we should be aware of its dangers and aware of its value. Throughout Buddhist literature we are taught that we should use words as skillful means for the alleviation of suffering and that we should not get stuck on their meaning or their bewitching power. The way we practice Zen is to put the emphasis on letting go of words, on sitting meditation that allows the mind to see words come and go and frees up some space between them, and on complete nonverbal attention to simple tasks, like putting the key in the door to your house. With this letting go of words as our basis, we also encourage people to think; we have classes, talks, and discussion groups where people can engage their thinking minds with their lives, their feelings, their communities, and the Dharma.

Buddha lived in a society where lofty religious language and ritual dominated the cultural landscape, and so these were generally heavily de-emphasized—though not abandoned—in the early Buddhist teachings. The teachings tend to show how to use the cognitive and meditative capacities of mind to let go of suffering, to use just enough grand magniloquence to keep us motivated, wholehearted, and big minded. There is room for some huge, mind-blowing language in this tradition, and I think it's good to make some room for it in your life. Big language can make your mind vast, expansive; it can help to draw your heart and mind together; it can crack open your narrow, regular day-to-day concerned, ever-churning quotidian mind; and it can blow open the doors of your preconceptions and limitedness like the endless, ancient, all-pervading wind that's blown through the human heart since before we had words. Please let go of figuring anything out and just read Lex Hixon's presentation of this passage from the *Prajnaparamita Sutra in 8,000 Lines*. This is a samadhi text; it's purpose is to elicit the liberated mind.

> One who exists solely as this boundaryless mind and heart of wisdom and love will not perceive difficulties simply because one never perceives separation, substantiality, or limit. The ease, freedom, and delight of Mother Prajnaparamita flows through the awareness of the bodhisattva, a constant reminder that no personal self exists substantially or independently... This principle of ontological transparency applies to every subjective or objective structure or process that can possibly be experienced by any consciousness. Thus the consecrated heart of love is identical with the clear mind of transcendent insight.

This teaching is here not to present the truth, but to blow your mind—to blow out the cobwebs and the stale air. It invites you to come out of the attic of your mind's endless story and step into the fresh air of the mountainside and find an old guy, sitting next to a grass hut in a patch of sun. Or perhaps you'll find yourself looking up from this book at your cat lazing on the arm of the couch, and you'll realize that this is unsurpassable, that there isn't something else, there isn't truth, or life, or happiness somewhere else, that you can't surpass this because this is it, here and now.

# 17

## Light on the Mountain

A SHINING WINDOW BELOW THE GREEN PINES...

High in the mountains all over Asia, the monks doing their meditative and ritual practices are not just far from the hurly-burly of the city and town—they're close to the green things growing, to the high slopes, and to the plunging valleys carved by rushing and trickling water.

The first Zen retreats I did were at Hokyoji Practice Community in southern Minnesota, set in a meadow at the foot of steep towering hills, where pines, oaks, and aspens make their home, where midsummer lightning bugs sing their silent flashing mating songs, where autumn coyotes raise their voices in raucous chorus as the evening sunlight fades across the far green hills. The buildings are small and the walking human figures smaller against the great verdant landscape. The windows shine soft and yellow in the darkness before sleep; a green grove of pines stands above the grave of Hokyoji's founder, Katagiri Roshi, high up on the hill.

I have been hiking and backpacking for many years. My mother is from Montana and so we have a long connection with the mountains there. Since I was a child, and still to this day, when I take the train to visit family in the summer and we enter the mountains, my heart rises. I sit in rapt attention as we round each bend, following the contours of the broad bases and the great shoulders of the high green ridges. After I had been doing Zen practice for a few years, I noticed that when I was out hiking there was a very similar quality of concentration, care, joy, and reverence among people out in the woods as I had found in our Zen community back home. It was as though the mountains were doing Buddhist practice for us, or Buddhist practice was helping us return to the mountains.

Many people I know have arrived at similar insights in places other than mountains: Minnesota's boundary waters, amid the lakes and hills; out in the desert in New Mexico; sailing far out in the ocean; or biking across the Great Plains. In each case, our human place in the great landscape was small, like "a shining window below the green pines." We were presented with something sublime, something vast: the place where our ancestors lived and with which we evolved. We tasted its beauty, and we sometimes tasted fear. On the plains you can see a storm come from a hundred miles away as the dark clouds start to mass on the horizon.

It's mesmerizingly beautiful; the wind shifts hard to the east, the flash and boom grow steadily closer, trees lean hard as leaves leap into the air. We retreat into the tent as the rain starts to roar across the dry ground, and a little fear rises in the throat as the tent whips and snaps in the tempest. We touch something vast and real, we see how small we are, our senses carefully attune to conditions.

It's good to spend time in places where the things that people have made and manipulated are fewer, and things that have evolved together over the millennia are everywhere we look. Since we developed alongside everything else, it's nice to spend time with our family: birds, bushes, deer, and insects; canyons, streams, hills, and plains. It's good to be reminded that all things are related, and it's nice to be where we can see more clearly just how beyond our command things really are. We can settle in to our mutuality and let go of the illusion of control.

We can paint a mountain, we can write a poem about a mountain, we can take a photograph, though we know nothing comes close to capturing it. It's good to do all those things anyway, to meet the mountain with our creative selves. Mountains and all of nature—blades of grass, lakes and streams, frogs and flowers—give us an opportunity to manifest the big, calm, attentive, loving mind that is held forth as the promise of Buddhism.

Indeed, they naturally tend to draw this mind forth. They invite us to be with them the way Buddhism invites us to be with everything.

A few years ago I started leading people on meditative backpacking trips in Montana. We do sitting meditation every day, we take care of our bodies and our camps, we walk, and we are quiet. We see countless astonishingly beautiful landscapes, we are afraid of bears, we have feet that hurt, we chant the "Song of the Grass-Roof Hermitage," we develop deep love and trust for each other, and we feel surges of affection and care for each living thing we pass by.

As a teacher, the thing that I come back to most is that this loving, careful, appreciative, astonished way of being is not dependent on the mountains. The mountains draw forth the state of mind, but that state of mind is always available. Our practice below the green pines can show us a way to be in the world that is humble, kind, attentive, and joyful, which we can carry back with us to our homes, our families, and our entire world.

# 18

## Zen Plays with Irony

---

JADE PALACES OR VERMILION TOWERS
CAN'T COMPARE WITH IT.

It's just a little hut, a little light on a hillside, and yet the grandest building you can imagine can't compare. Take a minute to really picture a jade palace: splendorous and immense, intricately carved from a soft, luminous, and precious stone. In Chinese mythology it is the residence of the emperor of heaven. Then we have an awe-inspiring tower of vermilion. This was written long before skyscrapers, when a tall building was an astonishing achievement. Now imagine one in a brilliant orange-red. Nonetheless, Shitou says these grand visions still are no match for our "shining window below the green pines." Our poet is playing with language here, playing with a key feature of Chinese Zen: irony.

Chinese Zen teachers often use irony—which in this case means saying one thing and meaning its opposite—to open up lots of room for engaging with a teaching. They might say one thing that sounds pretty good, that seems logical and wise, but its opposite also has some truth. Usually, either interpretation is limited— neither one is completely correct, but both have some truth. In Zen irony we often say one thing and mean both what we said and its opposite—and neither one. This is about using words to not get stuck on words, it's about being flexible, it's about stretching the limits of the mind.

In case 21 of the *Gateless Gate*, a classic collection of Zen stories, we find this account:

> A monk asked Yunmen, "What is Buddha?"
> Yunmen said, "Dried shitstick."

He's referring to sticks that were used like toilet paper in that bygone era. On one level, his answer is so profane and shocking that it seems to hold forth that Buddha, the question itself, and perhaps the questioner are utterly worthless. Really, what could be lower than a shitstick? Why on earth would someone who'd devoted his entire life to Buddhist practice and study say that? Perhaps to get us to release our fixations on some lofty being, the Buddha, or some lofty enlightened state that is somewhere else. Perhaps to try and get his contemporaries to let go of the formulaic questions and answers that were all the rage in Chinese Zen; perhaps to try and get the student to just wake up for a minute, to be in the moment, by shocking him.

If we look at his answer from another side, he's actually elevating the lowest possible thing to the highest level of veneration. He's saying, literally, a dried shit-stick is Buddha. He's telling us that going to the bathroom isn't wasted time; that's all that we have in that moment. When we throw away the most vile things, we try to view them with an open, venerating mind; when we see a dirty man with matted hair, blind drunk on the sidewalk, we should realize that what we conventionally put down as "below" us is actually Buddha.

One meaning says Buddha is worthless; it's just an idea you are stuck on. The other says that what you think of as worthless is actually Buddha, the most wondrous thing, to which you should devote your life. The basic message underlying both is to let go of comparing and open your heart to everything.

So when Shitou says "A shining window below the green pines—Jade palaces or vermilion towers can't compare with it," the most surface meaning is that towers and palaces are not as good as his little window; a little hut is better than the grandest achievement. I have tasted this, doing sitting meditation in a humble tent as darkness fell. The simplicity, the stillness, the quiet, the connection of mind to everything seemed complete. Just to be truly at peace was greater than any palace, accomplishment, or desire; there was nowhere else I would possibly have chosen to be.

However, this line can also be taken to mean that

these grand edifices and this lowly hut can't be compared because they are completely unique, absolutely different. When we compare things we don't actually see them as they are; we're seeing our mind's interpretation of them. When we do meditation we let the mind have a few breaks from comparing, and that is one of the reasons that meditation makes life seem so fresh, surprising, and dynamic; it helps us see things not in relation to our ideas about other things—but just see them. We can taste their complete, incomparable uniqueness.

On the other hand, the hut and the palace can't be compared because they are completely, inextricably linked; they are the same, one is not separate from the other. When a mind is trained by meditation it can sometimes let go of dividing up the world. The mind lets go of being a mind separate from other things. There is not a mind, or a hut, or tower, but just this, whatever it is, indescribable and undivided. We say we can't compare things because they are not things; they are not separate from one another.

The grandest things do not compare with our humble hut; all human achievement can't compare with the simple practice of meditation and kindness. I write this as encouragement. I believe it is incomparably good. And yet, it can't be compared to any other. In each moment, at each place, everything is utterly and completely distinct and unique, worthy of wholehearted care, and each thing is completely the same. All things just an unknowable, indescribable interbeing, manifesting connection.

# 19

## Protection, Shelter, Refuge

JUST SITTING WITH HEAD COVERED,
ALL THINGS ARE AT REST.

Again and again this poem returns to the theme of rest, ease, calm. Here Shitou reminds us of the value of refuge, that we can take shelter as part of our practice to help us realize this peace. After all, he's not sleeping outside; he's got a hut to protect him. Shitou says we don't need a lot: just something to cover our heads, our little ephemeral hut. Sometimes we need to concentrate on finding this sense of safety to have any hope of finding ease, and sometimes it may not be so difficult, but feeling safe is a fundamental human physical and psychological need.

Since the earliest days of Buddhism, when people make a commitment to the path, they have taken refuge:

> I go for refuge in the Buddha,
> I go for refuge in the Dharma
> I go for refuge in the Sangha.

These phrases have been chanted by many, many millions of people seeking peace through the practice laid out by the Buddha. We often chant them on retreats at the end of the day; in the dim light the soft, sweet, untrained voices of our community wend their way through the ancient words, and we feel safe, and calm, and quiet. Similarly, when we practice loving-kindness meditation using the ancient phrases from the earliest days, we say, "May you be happy and at peace, may you be safe and protected, may you be healthy and strong, may you be at ease." The relationship between feeling safe and being at ease is intimate.

Shitou feels safe with very little external support, but for some of us this is very challenging. Each one of us has a unique life situation that gives us unique triggers for anxiety, and we should take these seriously. If you don't feel safe, it's important to get the support you need. Maybe there are external things in your life that you need to change. Perhaps you need to let go of relationships with people that harm you or habits that keep you in unsafe situations, and probably you need to find a place where you can feel safe on a deep level and settle in. A good teacher and a good community of practice can provide this.

Shitou's satisfaction with his simple hut does point toward something important, though: the very human tendency to try and focus on getting things to create a sense of safety. Billions of dollars are spent to condition us to think we can buy the things we need to secure the safety of our happiness. People who are poor do suffer more fear and anxiety than those with enough money to have sufficient food, shelter, and medicine, of course. But once those basic needs are met, money's not worth much for promoting our well-being. There's plenty of recent scientific research to confirm this age-old piece of wisdom: all we need is enough to cover our heads.

To find safety, and to be well in all regards, Buddhism teaches us to take care of the basics of our external, material world and then focus on developing a mind that is free from fear. Sitting with your head covered refers not just to having a roof to protect you but also to the practice of meditation. By covering his head, he reveals the world; by dampening the dominance of the mind, he exposes the body and the senses. Covering the head leaves everything else out in the light; letting go of mental activity lets everything else be. Beata Grant, in her book *Daughters of Emptiness*, shows us how the great nun and poet Xinggang realized the close relationship between safety, meditation, and intimacy with all things:

> A single meditation cushion, and one is
>     completely protected,
> Earth may crumble, heaven collapse—but
>     here one is at peace.

Sacred titles and worldly fame: both fade
away in the sitting,
And the universe assembles on the tip of
a feather.

We shouldn't use our cushion to run away from the world, but sometimes we need a place of refuge. Sometimes we need a reminder that we are safe to be able to settle into the quiet and the completeness of our connection to things, to let all things rest, to see that in each tiny feather tip is the whole world ready for our wholehearted care and attention.

# 20

## Only Don't Know

I love learning; I was raised to read and inquire. So naturally when I was quite new to Zen, I read a lot of books. One day at my neighborhood library I checked out a book of recorded conversations and letters from the Korean-born teacher Seung Sahn, one of those teachers who first brought Zen to America. He favored koan practice, challenging students with difficult questions. Often after a round of confounding questions and answers the student would exclaim, "I don't know!" This was as likely as anything to elicit a positive response from the demanding Korean teacher, "Good, only don't know." In a sense, of course, not-knowing was a basic driver of my intellectual upbringing, for you can't be curious if you think you already know everything. This, however, was different; Zen recommended just remaining in, spending time with, and really being not-knowing.

Around the time I was reading Seung Sahn, I was

part of a support group for people who had family or close intimates who suffered from alcoholism. The main emphasis of this group was to help people take care of their selves and their responsibilities without being caught up in or trying to control the drama and difficulties of their alcoholic loved ones. As we'd sit in a small circle at noon in a dumpy church basement, people kept bringing up the same thing: they really had a hard time resting in not-knowing. They kept trying to control the people around them and their situations so they could have a sense of certainty, and it never really worked. This wisdom rose out of that group, but it is also one of the most central ideas of Mahayana Buddhism; human suffering is deeply related to the fear of uncertainty, the fear of not knowing.

We don't know how our kids will do in school, when a hurricane will flood the coast, when we'll fall into the same old emotional traps, when the economy will collapse or grow, how our partners will be feeling tonight—the list is endless. We don't know, but we focus so much time, heart, and attention on trying to figure out how to make things go the way we want, when we're actually ignoring the much bigger and more frightening unknowns: how long before we lose our health, when our parents will die, when we will die. "Between certainty and the real, an ancient enmity," said Zen teacher and poet Jane Hirschfield. No matter how hard we try to figure out and arrange things, they will always go their own way. Our suffering is just our disagreement with this uncertainty; it is the suffering of the dissonance, the enmity, between what we think we know and what is.

Not-knowing is a position of vulnerability and humility. "This mountain monk doesn't understand at all." Shitou doesn't tell us he's acquired some special knowledge; instead he's a simple man practicing simplicity. As my teacher sometimes tells me, "Just come back to zero." The spirit of this can open you up to people and ideas. When you see someone on TV voicing political ideas you abhor, can you even hear what that person says, or are you already creating an argument in your head that he or she will never hear? Can you see that the politician is just a person like you, trying to figure things out by making them go a certain way? This is a wonderful practice. I used to get so angry when George W. Bush came on the radio, then I decided to practice just listening without prejudice to his voice and what he was saying. As a result, I started showing up to work much less angry—which was nice for my students! It didn't slow me down from canvassing and volunteering for John Kerry; I just did it with a lighter heart.

The value of not-knowing does not mean that thinking is bad. Early Buddhism placed more emphasis on cognitive knowledge than many later strains, but almost all branches esteem it to some extent. Shitou and Dogen both encourage us to break beyond the bonds of what we know, but both do so from the context of vast personal knowledge of Buddhist literature. Knowing and not-knowing are both good, but many teachings emphasize not-knowing because avoiding or denying it is such a powerful human tendency.

Seung Sahn's phrase "only don't know" can be a reminder to us to open up a little bit, to let our selves touch uncertainty. The prajnaparamita sutras, which push the mind toward a radical not-knowing state, often mention that there is fear in stepping toward uncertainty. Letting go of the armor that our consciousness has evolved to construct is not always easy, but it is profoundly liberating. Sitting in a room full of meditators is the best place to find a sense of safety and really let go of what you know. When you breathe in, you can see that you're just breathing, and you can feel that everyone is there in a quiet place to support each other. Sometimes when you see that you are breathing, you may not see "breathing" but just sensations that are distinct, fresh, never known before. You may stand up after zazen and walk into an awakening city that's as new and wide open as the eyes of an infant child.

# 21

## Home Is Where You Are

LIVING HERE HE NO LONGER WORKS TO GET FREE.

### LIVING HERE

Where do you live? I usually answer that question, "In Minneapolis," or if I'm talking to someone local, "I live uptown," but neither of these are strictly true. More accurate would be to simply say that I live here. *This* is the place where our life exists. At our houses, biking down the street, in a long line in a grocery store, or boarding an airplane. Wherever you are right now, this is where you live.

Because we don't think this way, we generally feel like we're not at home, like we're not in our lives. If I live in Minneapolis, what am I doing in Duluth? If I live on Colfax Avenue, I'm apparently not really living when I'm riding down the tree-lined road to Saint Paul. Maybe it's time for us to decide to live where we are, instead of feeling split and trying to keep up from one place to the next—maybe it's time to live here.

I'm not suggesting we answer people's inquiries about the location of our homes with some deep Zen response: "I live here." *Gong*. I'm also not saying we need to let go of the idea of being part of a place, of belonging to a community. But let's play with words a little bit and open up the possibility of living completely wherever we are. Our mountain monk's "here" is his hermitage; he's not on retreat from some other place. He is fully in this place. Sometimes I'm very amused, and sometimes aggravated, when I see how often my mind is concentrated on being somewhere else. I may be walking down a street littered with golden fallen leaves in the sharp, crisp sunshine and be completely unaware of the beauty around me, instead imagining being at work, or in a meeting, or spending time with my son, or getting back to the mountains. I had no idea how much my mind did this until meditation became a regular part of my life; now I get to see it all the time.

In *Genjokoan*, Dogen only gives a few specific practice instructions: "Practice intimately and return to where you are." Later he says, "When you find your place where you are, practice occurs, actualizing the fundamental point." Realizing we are here is our practice, and practicing is realizing we are here. Practice is the Buddha Way.

What is here anyway? The clickety-clack of the keys on my keyboard, a plane's roar, patches of autumn sun through old warped windows, a faint hint of this morning's incense, a soft straight back on the chair my dad used to write in. Sight, sound, smell, taste, touch, and thought: that's what's here. These six are what Buddha called the All, not really as in "That's all there is," more like "That's all you've got to work with," or "Pay attention for a while, and see if you find anything other than this All." If you think there's something else that is outside of the All, it's a thought, which is part of the All. This teaching does not claim that there is nothing outside of our consciousness; it simply encourages us to focus on what's here in this moment because this is the ground for our practice, our potential for liberation.

I invite you to take a moment to just taste what is here, to get in touch with the All. Just be the six: sight, sound, smell, taste, touch, thought.

You can take these moments throughout the day. You're already living here, so why not *choose* to live here instead of pretending that you're not. Have you ever noticed that it feels a lot better to choose to do something—something that you have to do, no matter what—than to try and avoid it? That's our lives. Here we are, and our mind is trying to pretend that it's going to take us to a better place. It's like a guy who always has some incredible idea or investment that's going to change everything. He's always got ideas, he gets so hard to listen to, he seems anxious, he's never satisfied, he doesn't get that much done, really. Do you know this type of guy? I live with this guy in my head. Sometimes

I get frustrated with him, with thought, but often I just see this mind, this old friend, and let him sit down here, be heard, and naturally quiet down. He's just as much here as anything else, just a part of the All. He's living here, I'm living here, the ringing in my ears from tinnitus is here, the stack of books on the desk is here, my thoughts of you are here. Life is here and we are living here.

## NO GAINING IDEA

I'm not a very good Zen teacher.

I talk quite a bit about how beneficial meditation and compassionate action are. I talk about how they help those who practice them, how they alleviate suffering in those near them, how the reach of their benefit is unknowable. I talk about the hundreds of recent scientific studies demonstrating that meditation results in less anxiety, less of a sense of alienation, and increased well-being. I quote the Buddha: "More than your mother, more than your father, more than all your family, a well-trained mind brings greater good." I teach that meditation can improve things.

Good Zen teachers, on the other hand, say zazen is good for nothing. These teachers don't encourage us to practice by holding out the carrot of something better. They say this, right now, is it. As long as you look for peace someplace else, it will be someplace else. Consider this, from Heinrich Dumoulin's *Zen Buddhism*:

> Mazu was residing in the monastery of Dembo-in where he sat constantly in meditation. The master, aware that he was a vessel of the Dharma, went to him and asked, "Virtuous one, for what purpose are you sitting in meditation?"
>
> Mazu answered: "I wish to become a buddha."
>
> Thereupon the master picked up a tile and started rubbing it on a stone in front of the hermitage.
>
> Mazu asked: "What is the master doing?"
>
> The master replied: "I am polishing [this tile] to make a mirror."
>
> "How can you make a mirror by polishing a tile?" exclaimed Mazu.
>
> "And how can you make a buddha by practicing zazen?" countered the master.

There are countless layers of meaning, myriad interpretations to this koan, but one of the simplest is this: don't practice meditation to become something you are not. Trying to get to someplace else, some other state or some other state of affairs, is a problem. Using meditation for this purpose just rolls our practice up together with the pattern that was creating our suffering. This is why in Soto Zen we say, "Just sit." Don't sit for anything, or to do anything—just sit. Just sit means don't do anything more than just sitting; don't contemplate the Dharma, don't review your week, don't rehearse arguments with your spouse, just sit. However, just sit also means that there is only sitting, that there is not something other than sitting. That is to say, anything you think is separate from just sitting is not actually separate from just sitting; the separation is just a specious mental construction.

When we sit down to practice meditation, something interesting happens. Most of us see lots of thoughts come and go: we think about what's on the agenda for the day, we recall the lovely food we had last night, we wonder how soon the bell will ring so we can stand up and get our sleepy leg to wake up. Then perhaps we get annoyed at all these thoughts. We want to be just sitting, but instead here we are sitting and thinking. But this *is* just sitting; thoughts are not separate from just sitting, because just sitting is the state of not-separateness from anything that is always here whether we know it or not. If we make a serious commitment to just sitting we may realize this not-separateness, but it's nice to remember that it's always realizing itself anyway.

Several years ago I showed up for a *sesshin*, a traditional period of intensive meditation at our Zen center. I had the opportunity to sit in meditation for several hours and spend the day in deep silence, devoting myself to simply doing each thing with my whole heart and attention: just raising the spoonful of soup, just bowing, just standing in line outside the occupied bathroom. Unfortunately I had been part of an unpleasant argument with my girlfriend the night before. I was riled up. I was sitting still as a stone with the soft scent of incense and relentless thoughts about what I should say, or should have said, and how she was wrong. My chest was burning, my breath tight. The upstairs bell rang to summon me for a one-to-one meeting with my teacher. I quietly made my way past the still and silent figures of my seated friends and climbed the stairs. In the interview room I faced my teacher and said, "I'm just sitting and there's all these angry thoughts and I'm totally obsessing!" Tim said, "Good, good!"

Now if I didn't trust Tim and have a great relationship with him, I might have jumped up and hightailed it out of that crazy place. But he knew me, and I knew him. And he spoke with a trust that I could take the teaching: not somewhere else, just this. His teacher Shunryu Suzuki emphasized that we should practice with no gaining idea, that our practice is not to become something better but to be here.

We do not need to work to get free, to be something else. Chop wood, carry water. Ride bikes, diaper children. You don't need to work for freedom. Just do this.

# 22

## Host and Guests

On the surface this line is about humility and withdrawing from the competitive, status-based world that we all live in. Dig deeper, though, and Shitou is giving us instructions for meditation practice.

In the Chinese court and temples of his time, enormous amounts of energy went into ritual displays of power. The characters for "host" and "guest" in Chinese are the same as those for "lord" and "vassal." To host was to exercise power, to be a guest was to be lowly. Although our modern Western culture is less class-bound and less ritualistic than Shitou's, we Americans still go through our lives trying to gain and maintain power. We struggle for a little more money to buy ourselves status symbols, but does anyone really need a Lexus more than a Corolla? Could we be content with a simple bike? We work to move forward in our careers and gain more authority among our colleagues. We strive for power over our children and our spouses. There's nothing harmful about exerting yourself to advance in an organization so your talents can help more people, and nothing wrong with asserting yourself within your family. However, the self-centered tendency to act like our own opinions and achievements are the most important, to try and arrange the world so we are at the center, is not helping us. Shitou says he's not going to make a fancy temple hall or lay out brocade seats so he can lord over visiting monks and manifest his great wisdom. He's also inviting you to look at your mind. Who is it that's trying to arrange things just so?

Shitou is reminding us to stay humble and let go of our worldly worries, but he's also saying some interesting things about meditation. The first thing many of us do to prepare for meditation is to find an upright sitting posture, which sounds a bit like "proudly arranging seats." Jack Kornfield in his book *The Wise Heart* talks a good deal about nobility, about having the posture of a prince. This can be really helpful; having an upright posture and using these noble terms can help us to let go of feelings of shame and powerlessness, which is important and necessary if we are going to realize our potential to be available to the world. However, sometimes we go too far. I've definitely found myself sitting in my lovely half-lotus in the Dharma hall thinking about how great my posture is. This tendency is even more common in yoga practice, where postures can get very elaborate. Shitou is poking our little prideful balloon. If thinking of sitting like a prince helps you, that's good. If you are stuck there, that's not so good.

Shitou is also referring to the philosophical principles of host and guest. In Zen teachings, the host is associated with the absolute and may also be known as emptiness or as unknowable, undivided, nondualistic interdependence. It is closely associated with enlightenment and infinite compassion. The guest is the relative, or anything that is understood in relation to something else: I and you, hot and cold, love and hate, the observer and the observed. Generally speaking we experience life as a sequence of relative things happening, and much Buddhist practice points us toward seeing the absolute, the host—toward unfettered connection.

Most of us go through our lives trying to entice guests, or, as the Buddha often described it, chasing after sense pleasures. Experiences, thoughts, and feelings are all guests. The basic human condition is to try to acquire and keep the ones we want. Shitou asks rhetorically, who would do this? Why would we keep engaging in this unsatisfactory runaround? But he's also back to that old question: who is this person?

Shitou is giving you an instruction: find out who is doing this chasing, instead of focusing on the things you chase. Turn around the light to shine within. Learning about yourself in a psychological way is good, and a valuable part of the process of answering Shitou's question, but once you've identified parts of yourself, they're guests, they are objects being seen by an observer, and it may be time to let go of them. For example, say you're annoyed that your boyfriend never notices when the tub is dirty or cleans it. You're a good meditator, so you sit down to notice these thoughts and turn the light inward. You taste the tensions in your body, you experience your raw anger, and you remember how this is a mirror of the same fight your parents always had. The insight into the origin of the feeling and the experience of the emotions and bodily sensations of anger are helpful, but they are guests. We can let them go and come back to a little curiosity; who is it that is feeling and thinking these things? Who is host to all these guests?

The host, you may recall, is associated with the absolute, with emptiness, with enlightenment. This is a host many of us would really like to entice. Sometimes we show up for a long retreat in the chill of early morning and in us is a hunger, a fire to gain enlightenment. This can be good and some traditions encourage it. But other teachers don't; if you are trying to entice the host to come and be your guest, it's a guest. If enlightenment is a thing to be chased, it's relative, an idea we've made up about something. Enlightenment, the host, is none of these.

Don't try to entice guests. Ask, instead: who? If what

I sense, feel, and understand are guests, if my sense of "I" is a guest, then who is hosting? Who is the host to all these guests? Don't ask with your mind, and don't spend time on answers. Ask with your heart, ask with your posture, ask with bare awareness.

# 23

## Buddhism Is Meditation and Kindness

---

TURN AROUND THE LIGHT TO SHINE
WITHIN, THEN JUST RETURN.

There are seven characters in each line of this poem, and in this line four of them include the meaning "return" or "come back." Come back home to this hut, to this moment, this place, just this, return. Two of the other characters carry the meaning "shine." Remember that old gospel song, the one that went "this little light of mine, I'm gonna let it shine"? Let it shine here; return to the now and illuminate this moment with simple, radiant awareness. The remaining character means "with ease" or "calmly." Come back, let your light shine here, return to here, take it easy, come home. This is the most essential element of Buddhist practice. We keep coming back to this message because the mind keeps trying to take us elsewhere, which makes us feel cut off from what is, from our lives, which are actually here, at home, in this moment. Just return, and let the calm, wordless mind of awareness illuminate.

In his earliest teachings, Buddha points back again and again—he returns—to the first teaching he delivered: suffering and the alleviation of suffering through the practice of wisdom, kindness, and meditation. In numerous sutras he is asked all kinds of questions, some of them very complex, and he answers them all with the same teaching. Each time, he calmly returns and shines a little light on the situation. Each time, he reminds us of his basic message of alleviating suffering through kindness and meditation.

These two practices, kindness and meditation, are intimately related. In one sense, we can understand this line of the poem by saying that to meditate is to shine the light within and to practice kindness is to return. We retreat through meditation and we engage through loving-kindness. In the Ten Oxherding Pictures of the Zen tradition, the oxherd goes deeper and deeper into realization, into emptiness, and in the end he returns to the village with open hands and a smile. Like so much of Shitou's poem this line is a prism, however, for we can also understand shining the light through kind action and just returning through meditation.

In meditation we turn around the light to shine within in the sense that by finding some space between thoughts we shed a little light on our own consciousness. Then, because we are not completely entranced by thinking, we can see that thoughts are happening, we can see emotions as they come and go, we can become aware that we have a sense that there is an I that is looking out at things, observing. Through the light of meditation, we see an awful lot about what we call "ourselves" that we would otherwise completely miss. In meditation, though, we also just return, because we just keep coming back to what is. We return to moments of the senses, to the sunlight slanting across the white wall, the feel on our fingers of the pages of a book.

In the practice of kindness, our most basic ethic, we also turn around the light. If we take a moment to look within, we are able to see thoughts and emotions come up in the mind and we can see if they are motivating us to do something kind or unkind. When my son is late, if I don't shine the light within myself, I may just chew him out when he finally arrives. If I do turn around the light, I can see that I feel hurt, I can see how badgering him will not help either of us, and I may calmly tell him how I feel and ask him to please be on time in the future. We also just return in our practice of kindness, since our kindness is rooted in being present, in really seeing and relating to what is here—not being half-hearted or prejudiced, but open and fully engaged in just this.

If we follow this way, we can provide some lightness, some light, some ease, a sense of coming home to ourselves and those around us. We can come home from work and spread a little joy; we can be really present to our children and our partners whether they are cranky, distracted, sweet, loving, or however they happen to be. We can settle into our seat in meditation and just rest in seeing what is; we can come back to our places of work in the morning with a radiant warmth, a shining smile, and our ears attuned; we can turn around and return again to shine a light on just this moment, a place we've never been.

# 24

## What Do You Depend On?

THE VAST INCONCEIVABLE SOURCE CAN'T
BE FACED OR TURNED AWAY FROM.

Most of us have some things on which we feel dependent. We know we need the support of our families; we also need our jobs so we can have income. Perhaps we depend on music to carry us through tough times. If we pay attention and have some openness, we may see that when we drive we depend on the federal government, which funds road building and educates future engineers; we may see that when we eat we depend on a farmer's manual labor; we may see that we are dependent on the sun, on the water that falls from the sky, on multinational corporations that extract oil to fuel vehicles that transport food, and on love, without which no human would ever make it past the age of two. If we really turn our attention to those things that sustain us, we will never stop counting. Every atom in the sun, without which we'd be awfully cold, is burning away, an integral part of infinite happenings that support us.

When we look at things in this way we turn to face the source of our lives, without which we cannot be. This is a wonderful practice. From it flows gratitude, connection, and humility.

Often we are turned away. Most of us do this almost all the time. Our awareness of our dependence on other people, on water, air, fire, and earth, is nowhere to be found in our minds. Instead, we're planning. We're reviewing. We're rehearsing. We're absorbed in our own concerns. This is a common human condition and, it's important to note, largely a futile one; no matter how much we focus on figuring out and controlling things, how completely consumed by our current projects or concerns we are, our dependence is completely undiminished. Where we could see connection, we see alienation, where we could realize humility, we try and control, where gratitude could flow like the rivers to the vast and rolling sea, we feel alone. This is why much of our practice is to help us open up to our awareness that we are not operating alone but that instead we're part of a great interdependent unfolding and are always intimate with all things.

Shitou's point, however, is actually even subtler. He says, "The vast inconceivable source *can't* be faced or turned away from." When we turn our face toward our dependence on infinite conditions, toward the source that allows us to exist, we're turning toward an *idea* of that source, not the source itself. The true source is vast and inconceivable—it's beyond any ideas. We can't turn away from it, because it is always right here.

There's no way for the human mind to even begin to conceive what is needed for it to exist in this moment. If we try thinking about it, all we find is a limitless horizon: we depend on food, which depends on the sun, which depends on gravity, which depends on the interaction of space and time, and only Einstein could tell us what those depend on. If we try to turn away and pretend we control our world, the world always shows up and does its own thing anyway.

Buddha never taught that there is a "source"; he told his students that trying to find the ultimate source was not a fit use of time, not conducive to the alleviation of suffering. Shitou is sort of in agreement; he says there is one, but you can't find it since you can neither face it nor turn away from it. I think Shitou's idea of a source is not meant to prove something about how the universe works but instead is meant to foster a certain kind of mind, a certain kind of heart. By speaking of a vast inconceivable source, he creates a feeling of dependence on and connection to something open, something beyond thought, that sustains us. He's careful not to let us think we can find it, know it, control it, or own it. This line of the poem is to open us up completely, to crack open some unanswerable questions: Where does this moment of experience come from? How vast and beyond my conceptions is this?

Sometimes when I chant this line after meditation there comes a feeling in my heart and mind that is so big, so open, so not-separate, like a deep, cool spring of well-being, an endless source with no location. I've never experienced a belief in any god, but I think it might be like the feeling people with such faith have when they feel a quiet, prayerful connection. It is a wonderful warmth; it radiates big smiles on my face toward passersby on the tree-lined street that lies between our Zen center and my home. It comes and goes, but it always seems to open up my heart. I don't look into this feeling for messages, directions, or meanings. This pretty clearly isn't something that's supposed to help me figure things out. I can't make it happen and I can't stop it from happening. It's not something other than what I'm doing; I can't know it, but I'm not separate from it. I depend on it.

# 25

## Meeting Our Teachers

As we near the end of his poem, Shitou begins giving us some instruction. A few lines ago he started by advising us to turn around the light to shine within and then return, to meditate and practice kindness. Now Shitou advises us to meet our ancestors, to become intimate with the wisdom of the great teachers throughout Buddhist history.

The practice of students and teachers meeting one to one, mind to mind, heart to heart, is central to the Zen tradition and is carried out every day in temples and practice centers around the world; authority to teach is given to students from warm hand to warm hand. Many old Chinese teachers refer to Zen as "family style"; the character translated as "familiar" here also carries the meanings "family," "parents," and "intimacy." We are encouraged to engage with our teachers and with the great body of teaching texts as our family: with lots of

love; with commitment; with imperfections, aggravations, and disagreements; with a deep knowing that is
born of time together. We are not encouraged to simply follow instructions but are instead told to meet the
texts with our whole selves.

The written record of Zen is mostly koans and poems.
Koans are generally very brief, terse stories of conversations between Buddhists, usually (but not always) a
Zen teacher and a student. They show us some things
about this "family style": that practice and teaching one
to one is really valuable, that finding answers is not the
point, that asking questions is good. They can be quite
baffling. Koans are often densely allusive, referring to
esoterica that is buried in time, but more importantly
they create a multitude of possible interpretations.
The key element of koans is that they show us a tradition of using words, inquiry, and teaching that does not
offer us a fixed and correct answer but instead provides
a big, open space for us to enter and meet the matter in
question. Sometimes when we look at a koan we'll have
a strong, clear sense of its message, and often when we
use koans for teaching purposes we'll narrow its range
of meaning down to make a useful point, but a new day
or a new person may find a whole new field of possibility in its glittering ambiguities. Dogen's commentaries
on a koan, for instance, will often go from explications
of the wonder and genius of its teaching to pointing

out its terrible flaws; these are delightful examples of how to love and revere something and then laugh and critique it, to be devoted but not attached.

Zen poems tend to put a little bit less emphasis on multiple and conflicting layers of meaning. They often carry a more personal note, and they more frequently have a fresh air of encouragement for our practice, but they still present a wide space for meeting them with our own minds. This book, for instance, is about you and me and Shitou meeting. I have not set out to explain what Shitou means or to unpack each detail of each allusion he makes. When I sit down to write I'm meeting the text and I'm meeting you; my intention, my motivation, is to allow us all to have some time together. I know there will be things about this book that you'll disagree with. I'm pretty sure Shitou would be able to point out many things in this book that he thinks are not helpful. That's good. A family where there are never any conflicts or differences is probably a family that has some pretty troubling issues. I've got enough love for this tradition and received enough healthy support from my teacher and community that I can step out here as I am, with all my flaws, and meet you.

Koans often show students presenting themselves to their teachers in a very vulnerable way. I'm often struck by how brave they are, going in with their questions to their teachers, many of whom were very demanding. Zen creates a context where you can really put yourself out there and be who you are completely. We don't all have families like this, I know, but the hope is that Zen's "family style" makes room for us to be wholly who we are, while loving our whole tribe.

A couple mornings ago I was sitting in a circle with some of my sangha members in our lovely third-floor classroom, where the ravens perch just outside the window in the treetops. We were studying the Vimalakirti Sutra, in which the mythical layman Vimalakirti points out major flaws in the understanding of all of Buddha's first disciples. Some of us talked about how Vimalakirti seemed arrogant and unkind, how he was using his intelligence to assert superiority over others; others talked about how he was helping people see through their deep-seated attachments. We met each other and we met the teachings. We were not called together in this tradition to follow a perfect teaching to the letter but to engage our whole hearts and minds in inquiry.

When you read the words of the Buddha, or you hear someone teaching, you might say that you are *receiving* the teachings, but I think it's better to know that we are *meeting* the teachings. When we meet the teachings we are engaged—not passive. We are part of a process, a tradition, that includes using words to help us be free. It is not necessary to engage by providing a running verbal critique of what you are hearing or reading; that's actually avoidance. We meet the teaching by offering our whole attention, our whole selves, to the experience happening moment to moment— just as we can meet all things.

# 26

## Don't Give Up

BIND GRASSES TO BUILD A HUT,
AND DON'T GIVE UP.

After years of teaching introductory meditation classes, I can say one of the things I hear the most often from students is that they've wanted to have meditation be a regular part of their lives for years. I recall one student, who I'll call Ann, who sat face to face with me in the early morning light, showed me all the pain and aggravations of her life, and told me of her deep sense that meditation and a connection to a Buddhist community could help her free her mind from its constricting habits, the root of her suffering. She told me that for years she had tried to make a commitment to meditation, but she had always stepped away from it. An old Zen story tells of an emperor who visited a great Zen teacher and asked what the fundamental point was. The emperor waited for the deep and abstruse Zen response. Instead, the teacher answered, "Do that which is good, do not do that which is harmful." The emperor was annoyed, "Even a child knows that!" "Very good," responded the teacher, "then do it." Sometimes we don't know what the best thing to do is, but an awful lot of the time we know and just don't do it.

The characters in this line of the poem, translated here as "don't give up," could very well be translated instead as "don't back off." Don't back off from the challenge of your deepest aspirations, don't back off from what is here right now. To really see what life is in this moment, to devote ourselves to being well and helping others: these are challenges the mind is not habituated to take on. It takes courage just to sit down and meditate. It's not easy to sit down and really look at how completely out of control our thinking is. It's hard to sit and be really intimate with our emotions. It's hard to have faith that just sitting still and feeling the rise and fall of our bellies as we watch thoughts and sounds come and go is a profoundly generous act of service to the world. It's hard to have faith that letting go of our fixed views and cultivating a mind that has some openness to whatever arises is good for all of us. We get busy, we get anxious, we get pissed off, we get excited about something we want and we back away from what's here and retreat into our mind's projections—we give up. But we can always come back; trying again only takes a moment. This is the one.

At our Zen center we have practice periods every spring and fall. For eight weeks a big group of people make formal commitments to meditation practice, retreat, group study, mindful work, and kindness. At the beginning of our weekly meetings we go around the circle and check in with each other to see how we're doing with our commitments to practice. It's quite common for people to say that they haven't done as much sitting meditation as they had planned because they got very busy. A few years ago, however, my friend Matt said, "I'm extremely busy with a couple of big projects. I've got an album coming out soon, and I just got my first job scoring a theater production, plus my full time job, so I'm going to do a little more meditation than I planned to help it all go well." This statement seemed so completely bizarre and so exactly right. I have never spent so much time sitting that I wasn't able to get my other obligations done, but the more I commit to practice the better everything in my life goes.

Everything changes, and certainly a time may come when we may need to move on from Buddhism, or it maybe be true that we're not yet ready to begin a practice. If we're moving on because we know in our heart another path is right for us, that's good. But we need to investigate why we're doing this. Are we backing off from something really important to us? Are we giving up just because we're discouraged or unmotivated? We may run into emotional roadblocks, our teachers may disappoint us, perhaps we move away from our community of practice, or maybe we're busy with children. We may just keep cracking open the laptop and scrolling through Facebook pages instead of meditating. I know there's only so much time in a day and we all make our own choices about what's best. You may only have a little bit of your life to give to Buddhist practice. That's okay. The message here is don't give up on the present moment, don't give up on what really matters to you. Your capacity to grow and help others is unlimited; you have gained the pivotal opportunity of being human. Find the support you need, find a way that is kind to you to support yourself, to support those you love, to grow the circle of those you love. Don't give up and don't back off from the once-in-a-lifetime opportunity shining in this moment.

I see Ann almost every weekend now in between meditation and our Dharma talk. We share big smiles, and sometimes we sit down and she talks about her beautiful sense of connection to nature and her struggles to keep meditation a regular part of her life. She's told me it's hard to sit down on her own at home, but it's not hard when we all do it together.

# 27

## Freedom from the Past

LET GO OF HUNDREDS OF YEARS AND
RELAX COMPLETELY.

### KARMA

Do you ever feel like you've got a thousand years on your back?

When things seem so heavy, it's because we're carrying around too much time; we need to come home to the now and lay down all that weight, all that time. To "let go of hundreds of years and relax completely" is to let go of holding on tight to the limiting concerns of our limited lifetimes, to let go of the long, long string of our worries and hopes and take a moment of ease. It is to be free of our karma.

Karma is about the relationship between what's happened, what will happen, and what we choose right now. Sometimes we say karma just means cause and effect, but it's a complex concept that means very different things to different people. Instead of addressing all the various ways of understanding karma today,

I'm just going to talk about a way people in my practice community use and understand the concept—I'm going to talk about an understanding of karma that can help us relax completely.

Suppose you are walking down a street. The sun is rippling across the sidewalk through the breeze-blown leaves that rustle overhead, a dog is smelling a lamppost, the scent of grilled meat is thick in the air, your pace is quick but easy. As you cross a street, a car appears, coming fast, straight for you, and screeches to a stop a few feet away. What is occurring in your body and mind? Many responses are possible, though the tendency to experience fear in a situation like this is almost universal. Fear's principal, primal function is to respond much faster than thought to dangerous stimuli; it fills us with adrenaline so we can leap away from danger. It is the result of very old karma—millions, not hundreds, of years of accumulated tendencies of body and mind, developed through evolution. When we experience fear or anger we are experiencing very deep karma; people have been carrying around the body and mind equipment that creates these feelings for as long as there have been people.

Along with fear, as we stand in the street shaking and looking at the shining mass of metal near our thighs, we are likely to experience changing emotions and thoughts. Perhaps we are angry: where did this moron learn to drive?! Perhaps the fear dominates and we are shaken up for hours. Perhaps we experience compassion, realizing that the fear running through our body is an unpleasant sensation, aware that the person in the car is probably experiencing something similar.

Whatever story is created in our mind by this occasion, it's usually all we see. When we're angry with the other driver, we can be completely absorbed in the narrative we create about his ineptitude and irresponsibility. When we're frightened for our lives, we fixate on the dangers around us, on how death can lurk at every turn. However, if our mind is trained in meditation, sometimes we just see the thoughts and feelings come and go, and we can see that they do this on their own, that they are just our conditioning, our karma, doing its thing.

After your initial response of fear, the emotions you experience in a situation like this have a lot to do with what happened to you earlier in the day. If you yelled at your kids, who wouldn't get up in the morning, and you spilled coffee all over your shoes, and you hate Mondays, and *then* you almost got hit by a car, aren't you a little more likely to be angry than if you got up and did an hour of meditation and went for a walk with a friend to talk about how to be more kind? In the same way, your reaction also depends on the last few years; are you living in a way conducive to anger or kindness? If you spend a decade listening to angry people on the radio, you are more likely to experience anger than if you spent that time listening to birdsong. Similarly, your response is also dependent on how you were raised. People who grew up in a family with a lot of fear and violence, for instance, have very different reactions to fear and violence than those who don't. The patterns of behavior and reactivity that we carry are intimately connected to how we were raised, how we've chosen to live, how our parents were raised, and how they chose to live. That's our karma, that's how hundreds of years show up in each moment, how our experience of the world is a projection of our conditioning.

Karma is a very, very old idea. One of Buddha's innovations was his emphasis on karma as caused by volition, by intention, not just action. Each moment of our lives, our consciousness presents us with an opportunity for volition: a choice. Much early Buddhist teaching is about directing our energy and attention toward our intention in each moment, turning our purpose toward the alleviation of suffering. If you consider that each moment of consciousness is the product of hundreds, actually millions, of years of karma, then what you choose now is part of the process that creates the ground for the rest of your life and the lives of everyone else. It's all connected. The effects of shouting at someone go on forever for you and everyone else—so do the effects of smiling.

To let go of hundreds of years is to bring our mind to this moment; we let go of the burden of our worries about the past and the future. Sometimes this moment is not such an easy place to be. If we're anxious, sad, or angry, resting in that emotion can be hard, but if we just stay we can ease into and realize that this moment of difficulty is nowhere near as troubling as the long story that our mind is ready to create, which will try and fix the difficulty but actually perpetuates it. When we bring our mind to this moment we can let go of our karma, we can actually respond consciously to what's here rather than just manifesting our karmic conditioning.

Letting go of the hundreds of years of conditioning we carry by actually seeing this moment with our whole selves, we find ease. When we make the choice to alleviate suffering, we can straighten our backs and relax completely.

## RELAX COMPLETELY

If there's one theme of this poem, it's that we should feel encouraged to relax, to be at ease. People very often think that relaxing is something we do for ourselves, that it is selfish, but if everyone in the world was a little more relaxed, wouldn't the world be a better place? Wouldn't people's home lives be better? Wouldn't the dialogue between conservatives and liberals be better? Wouldn't the experience of traveling from home to work be better? Sure, maybe the most ambitious of us wouldn't achieve quite so much; it's possible that if everyone in the world were more relaxed we'd have fewer people pushing the limits of the human body in sports or exploring the frontiers of knowledge in the sciences, but I'm not so sure. I have seen some remarkably relaxed people devote huge amounts of time, talent, and effort to the arts, Buddhist practice, and service to their communities. I think it's important to remember that relaxing is an act of kindness.

What do you do to relax? I asked a group of kids this question at the juvenile detention center here in Minneapolis, while I was leading a meditation group there. Reading, listening to music, playing basketball, smoking pot, and meditating before bed all came up. Some of these ways are better than others. If what we do to relax works at the time but causes problems down the road, it's not a very good method. Sometimes we can't always see when something we do causes harm; this is why paying attention and being open to other people's ideas is important. I personally have seen smoking pot take a horrible toll on many people's lives; for instance, it was the reason the person who mentioned it in that little circle at juvenile detention was incarcerated. She didn't like being in the detention center at all, so I suggested she could find some other ways to relax that were less likely to end up with her incarcerated. Another example is reading, which can be a wonderful way to relax, but I know people who've had to learn to let go of it a bit when they realized that they were using it to escape reality. They always had to put the book down eventually and life was still there.

In Zen, our practice of meditation is about being completely here, with what is—not withdrawing into a transcendent place. Meditation is not about getting something for ourselves. It is possible to turn meditation into a selfish act. We have to look into our own hearts and hear those around us to make sure we're not getting out of balance. Making a commitment to relax completely is good, but make sure this doesn't come from a selfish place, that it comes from a sense of connection, and that it stays connected to your values and those around you.

Picture in your mind a great symbol of relaxation. Perhaps one of those ads on the television where people are lazing in lounge chairs under an azure sky, amid the low, rhythmic pulse of the sound of waves on the soft pale sand. I love relaxing on the beach. This morning I sat on the sand next to the lake near my home with my jacket on and a cool breeze off the lake, listening to gulls and geese calling to each other as they headed south. Unfortunately, not even the most idyllic setting can create calm in a mind habituated to suffering. Quite a few years back I went on a family vacation to a beach town in Mexico, which half of my family spent in a nasty argument that had them completely on edge. Trying to go somewhere or arrange things so we can relax might help, but really what matters is our mind.

This idea is so central to Buddhist thought: by taking compassionate care of our mind we can reduce suffering. The practice of meditation and kind action, which is the root of Buddhism, is a way of relaxing. To be at ease is the Way, and it is the fruit of the Way.

Each moment is an opportunity to let go, and the possibility is there in every situation to relax completely. However, trying to *make* ourselves relax doesn't work so well, does it? I've had some hilarious inner dialogues during meditation retreats, trying to force my mind to be at ease. That just won't work. To relax completely is to allow things to be as they are—and that includes ourselves. I recall lying on my back in a yoga pose during a retreat once, and the person leading our yoga said, "Let go... Let go of letting go." Something opened up in me.

To relax completely is to allow things to be as they are, and that includes ourselves. However we are, we can allow that to be; we can relax around it without trying to control it. Moment to moment, we can open up to what's here, including all the difficulty and the tension, the elation, or the boredom. We relax completely not by causing something to happen but by allowing what is to be, without judgment or control.

# 28

## Lay Down My Sword and Shield

OPEN YOUR HANDS AND WALK, INNOCENT.

An open hand grasps nothing; an open hand lets go. This letting go has a close relationship to nonharming; in many ancient cultures an open hand showed that you held no weapon, that you meant no ill. An open hand grasps nothing, and when we hold on to nothing we are letting go.

When we do no harm we are in a state of innocence. The characters in Shitou's poem translated here as "innocence" mean "without crime"—and also mean "without punishment." Thus, the language shows us the intimate relationship between doing harm and suffering. This is karma: what we do, say, and think patterns the future. If we do harmful things, we suffer. If we do kind things, we find some peace.

The character for "walk" here also means to conduct oneself or to practice, to do. Often in Zen it is used in contrast to the idea of turning the lamp inward—to walk is to go forward into the world. Shitou continues to investigate the balance between meditative practice and engagement. Here, he advises us to go out into the world without harming, without grasping, and humbly show that we are vulnerable.

Long ago people invented weapons, and they're still at it. People will speak of using weapons to defend themselves as a separate and distinct act from using weapons for aggression, but at root they are closely related. A weapon is a tool whose creation and use is motivated by fear or aggression, by an attempt to try and make things go our way. Fear and the impulse for protection, as well as aggression and the impulse to attack—fight and flight—are governed by very similar physiological systems in the body and feel very similar if we actually attend to experiencing them: the heart races, the body gets hot, cognition gets cloudy, but the limbs move fast and powerfully or are intensely, powerfully still. Some people are more conditioned to experience one or the other, to extremely varying degrees, but we all feel both to some extent. Many of us today experience both fear and aggression simultaneously on a low level much of the time. We're worried about how we're perceived at work, and we resent a coworker who competes with us; we're annoyed by our misbehaving children and concerned for their future; perhaps every time a certain political figure comes up in conversation we make snide remarks. So our body might be running a little hot on the fear-anxiety-worry-anger-hatred-aggravation meter.

Even if we don't own any literal, physical guns or swords, we all have our weapons. We have our tools that we use when we're running hot to try and make things go our way. Maybe we have excellent sarcasm skills to deploy in meetings to cut people down, or maybe we withhold affection from our loved ones, or maybe we talk about people behind their backs. If we want to "walk, innocent," if we really want to be free of the suffering that leads us to hone and wield our weapons, we need to open our hands and lay them down.

In order to release our weapons, it's first necessary to see them; this is one reason that we meditate, to see what our mind tends to do. If we see these weapons, we will also see our suffering that makes us want to use them, and if we lay them down we can see ourselves yet more clearly—and so can everyone else. When we open our hands we may feel some fear at being exposed, but we can find vast freedom in not constantly waiting for a fight.

There are many situations where taking decisive action to defend yourself is necessary. In the face of physical violence or verbal abuse we need to get away to safety. However, in most cases where we are aggressive or defensive, our reactions are completely unhelpful. I had a colleague who'd many times done and said things that I thought were harmful. When I thought of her or saw her, I would tense up, and I would be guarded and aloof. Eventually I got tired of being so tense, so I started practicing meeting her as if for the first time, without the armor I'd built up from the past; I let go of trying to tightly control our relationship, and I listened closely. I found that she was often quite kind, I started to learn of her own life's difficulties, and when she was unkind or gossipy it stopped sticking in my craw. I learned how to stop taking her difficulties and turning them into negative feelings.

"If you have no wound on your hand, you can touch poison without being harmed. No harm comes to those who do no harm." So says a line from the Dhammapada. Clearly, when a stray bullet strikes a child in one of the impoverished neighborhoods in my town, this phrase does not ring true, but it points to something powerful. If we lay down our weapons, open our hands, cultivate nonharming, we will find that all those things that we were afraid of, all those things we hated or drove us nuts, do not harm us anymore. It may take some time to adjust to not having our defenses, and it may be hard, but this is the ground for a beautiful, peaceful, and powerful engagement with the world. We can conduct ourselves in a world full of dangers, difficulties, and injustice without contributing to the problems and without being overwhelmed by them.

The other morning I met with someone new to Zen practice, and she observed that it was "almost impossible not to be overwhelmed when you start doing some kind of charity work." She had been taking in rescue cats and her whole house was arranged to accommodate seven troubled cats who hated each other. And, of course, there were still hundreds more in the shelters. It occurred to me that Zen practice is basically about cultivating and manifesting the possibility of completely giving yourself to being of service, even in the face of insurmountable difficulties, with a sense of ease. This ease grows out of our innocence, out of our commitment, cultivation, and practice of nonharming and kindness. It lets us walk into a world where people are killing each other, starving, hopelessly lonely, driven by anger, or homeless—or simply lets us come home to a cranky spouse—and be available, kind, and attentive without being swept away.

This is about walking the walk—about walking the Way. This is about being able to sit in a tense and combative meeting and be at peace and offer helpful words. This is about giving an apple to a homeless man because you know what hunger feels like. This is about waking up and realizing that you don't care about getting that new phone, but you want to help fund a water project in Ethiopia. This is about watching your child struggle in school and just being available, attentive, and supportive. We can do these things and be at peace. We start by opening our hands, learning to let go of harming, and stepping out as we are, innocent.

# 29

## The Joys of the Human Mind

With all the talk about being free of concepts, letting words and the storytelling mind fade away, and wholeheartedly engaging in activities, one might imagine that language is the enemy of the freedom, compassion, and joy offered by Buddhist practice. But the Zen tradition is not about living without words; it's about not being utterly consumed and bewitched by them. This poem tells us to know the teachings, to "meet the ancestral teachers, be familiar with their instruction," but not be ensnared by them.

Zen in particular emphasizes the value of nonthought. One of the earliest teachings of Zen was the declaration by Zen's near-mythical founder, Bodhidharma, that his realization was a "direct transmission, outside the scriptures, with no dependence on words and letters." Of course, he used words to give this teaching, and it's also said that Bodhidharma carried with him a copy of the Lankavatara Sutra, a lengthy and very intellectually complex treatise on mind and enlightenment. He didn't cast words out—he just used them sparingly, and he was firm in his conviction that enlightenment was not something that could be contained in a document, that there is no ultimate truth that can be written down.

"Thousands of words" is quite an understatement; this book alone has over thirty thousand of them and this is one of countless books. The capacity of the human mind to generate words and thoughts is truly amazing. Nothing makes this more apparent than meditation practice. When we direct the mind toward the breath, or sound, or sensations in the body, we get to see really vividly how much thought the mind makes. My teacher has given me countless reminders to not see thought as the enemy; I can get very frustrated with sitting for hours while my mind throws up the same stories again and again. I've come to view the profusion of thought like a dear nephew: familiar, surprising, beloved, frustrating, hilarious, and most importantly free to come and go.

In the next line of the poem, Shitou says that all these words "are only to free you from obstructions." Can we see that these thoughts that come and go are part of, not separate from, the process of our liberation?

Zen and other Mahayana teachings emphasize the value of nonconceptualization, of seeing how language divides and narrows our relationship to the world. Right view, the first step on the Eightfold Path, is often described in Zen as nondual awareness: no oppositions, no subject and object, no thought and no thinker, nothing that language can accurately describe since defining inherently creates opposites.

The early Buddhist view of right view is quite different; earlier traditions of Buddhism were much less wary of the perils of thought. In one well-known sutra Shariputra, known for his wisdom and skill in teaching, explains right view as knowing what is wholesome and unwholesome, knowing the Four Noble Truths, and knowing the twelvefold chain of dependent co-origination. These are complex teachings that are explained in great—verbal—detail. Shariputra encourages us to know them deeply and intuitively on a level beyond thought, but he also teaches us to know the words and to use them. Buddha famously instructed his disciples not to hold on to the teachings but to use them to cross from suffering to nonsuffering and then to let them go. However, in many more sutras he instructs them to memorize, deeply understand, and practice his verbal teachings.

So this is about a balance. Immersing yourself in Buddhist teachings may be a wonderful support to your deepest intentions. It's also possible that it will just help your mind build up ideas that make you feel separate. If you think Buddhist teachings are the Truth, that's probably a bad sign. Eventually someone you know, or a circumstance of your life, is going to present a different idea of truth. Sometimes I have to catch myself when something that comes from my Buddhist training seems painfully and obviously true to me, but the person I'm talking to sees it a different way. My practice is to let go of the ideas and instead really commit to meeting the person and myself where we are.

If you think Buddhist teachings can be helpful, I think that's pretty good. They sure seem to have been beneficial for me. Many times when I was faced with something tough, my mind has offered a little nugget of teaching that I read or heard somewhere, and it helped me to calm down, open up, and be kind. Sometimes really diving into some Buddhist text has cracked open my heart and let a great flood of love and light pour in.

I remember reading a book by Chogyam Trungpa years ago, before I even started meditating. I was in a tent in the desert at dawn. It was cool and my brother had just got the campfire going so the smoke smell was wafting into my little home. I read something about how our selves are just ideas that we have and that we are actually just a completely interdependent manifestation of everything. I unzipped the fly of my tent and stepped out into a sense of vast, unknowing wonder, and not long after, for the first time, I pulled a pillow off the couch and onto the floor and sat still and silent for a little while, without words, truly tasting the body breathing.

# 30

## One Taste

ARE ONLY TO FREE YOU FROM OBSTRUCTIONS.

In the words of Buddha, "Just as in the great ocean there is but one taste—the taste of salt—so in this teaching and discipline there is but one taste—the taste of freedom." You can jump in at Rockaway Beach in New York City or Muir Beach in Marin, you can swim the English Channel or boat from Bali to Cancun, but whether you dive in or fall in, whether it seems the waves will never let you up or you are calmly floating in the warm, sustaining sea—take a little sip of that water and you know where you are. Sometimes towering rocks line the shore and sometimes soft, pale sand, sometimes the ocean is scary beyond comprehension and sometimes it feels like coming home, but this strong salty savor never leaves. There are countless Buddhist teachings and some may seem to completely contradict each other, but finally, their root taste is freedom, freedom from disagreeing with what is.

Freedom means a lot of things to a lot of people,

but here we're talking about being freed from wanting things to be other than they are; we're talking about freedom from dukkha, dissatisfaction, suffering. "Thousand of words, myriad interpretations are only to free you from obstructions" means the teachings' only value is in creating this freedom. If they are not serving that purpose, let them go. If you are using them to help you win an argument, to feel like you are right, let them go. If you are using them to rationalize harmful behavior, let them go. If they are making you feel further apart from others, let them go. Set them free so they can be freeing.

What are obstructions? Anything that stands between everything operating in beautiful, mutually beneficial harmony. For instance, if we're driving to work and we're late and the off-ramp we need is closed, we may think that the road barriers are obstructions, and of course they are, but we can use some teachings to be free of them. Bringing the attention to the breath and the body, we can taste our aggravation about being late and see the thoughts that come into our mind. We can refrain from harsh speech and focus on taking care of our suffering. We can see that the biggest obstruction to our freedom is our habitual emotional response to not getting what we want when we want it. Just seeing this is actually a vast entranceway into freedom. Practice in this way and sometimes you'll find that when you see those road barriers you'll realize that they are not obstructing anything. They are just where they are. Their "obstruction" is just a concept based on your idea that you'd be able to drive up that ramp this morning. Instead, it's you and the road barriers today, and nothing's in the way.

Here's a little poem I wrote on retreat a few years back:

> Ground fog on Hokyoji
> Nothing is obscured
> it's just fog.

Many Buddhist teachings emphasize processes like this story of the road barriers. They instruct us to focus ourselves on how our mind is constructing our suffering, to refrain from actions that perpetuate the suffering, and in the moment to find insight and a little freedom. Over time if we repeat these practices our mind becomes less habituated to constructing dissatisfaction. Meditative practice and ethics remove roadblocks in both an immediate way and the long term by unbinding the habits that construct them.

Other teachings—of our myriad interpretations—make startling, sometimes interrogative, comments like "How can something be an obstruction? Who put anything in your way?" Instead of encouraging you to attend to elements of your consciousness like thought, feeling, and sensation, these teachings just do whatever they can to snap your consciousness into something completely immediate, free of any distinctions. If you just completely drive the car, those barriers aren't in the way. You know not to drive into them, so you drive where traffic is flowing. These teachings don't give us a technique so much as baffle us or jar us out of our stream of habitual thought and into our immediate activity. Amusingly, we often try and figure them out, so they end up being a barrier, an obstacle keeping us from seeing how our mind likes to have things figured out.

Two different teaching methods, one taste of freedom. All the countless ways to practice, everything you learn in the Buddhist tradition, every mindful breath you've taken: they are freedom. Freedom from obstructions is freedom from what cuts you off from a limitless expanse of connection. This is a freedom from struggling to control things; it is a freedom that opens you up to your completely unknown capacity to benefit everyone around you. This is freedom from the self-centered habits that prevent you from living purely as a manifestation of a vast, incomprehensible web of connection, of giving your life to what is.

# 31

## Timeless Intimacy

When you chant or recite this poem, you are the narrator; you are the person in the hut.

I've worked as a musician for many years. A while back someone observed that when I perform, I show the emotional tone of the songs I sing with my whole body; he asked whether this was because I thought of myself as playing the character of the narrator of the song. This was a puzzling question to me. On examination, it seems to me that when I sing a song, I *am* the narrator; I'm not just playing a part. When you say this poem's words, can you see that the "I" that has built a grass hut is you?

We can think of the grass hut in many ways, but one way is to view it as our self; that is, the temporary assemblage of experiential bits that we think of as a self. We build this little shelter to construct a sense of safety amid the incomprehensibly powerful, ever-changing weather of the world. Psychologically speaking, by acknowledging that we are part of its building and that it is frail we open the possibility of freedom. Building a solid sense of self is a crucial part of human development. But afterward, we have the potential to see that this sense of self is just that—a sense, not a truth—and that beyond it, around it, and in it everything is infinitely interconnected or inter-penetrating. By acknowledging that we took part in the building of the hut and by realizing that it is frail, we open the possibility of freedom.

According to the stories of the Dhammapada, when Buddha experienced enlightenment he said, "House builder, you have now been seen. You shall not build the house again." He saw through his tendency to build a sense of a self that was separate from other things, and he let it go. Thus he let go of all the anxiety, anger, and desire that accompany feeling separate from the rest of the world. This poem plays with that image from the Dhammapada a bit. Rather than seeing through the house builder and putting him out of work, Shi-tou just builds a place that's so simple he won't become attached to it.

Now, though, he says there is someone undying in the hut, and he's inviting you to meet that person. Do "you want to know the undying person in the hut"? Shitou wrote the poem, Shitou built the hut, he actu-ally lived in it. He got hot in the summer there. In the winter he got cold. He's saying, "If you want to know

me, here's what to do," and he's saying, "I am undying."
He's offering a way for us to meet completely; this is
the invitation Zen teachers have held forth for fifteen
hundred years: complete intimacy.

But wait: if you built the hut, and you're narrating
this poem, then you are the undying person in the hut.
You are Shitou. But none of this can be right, because
the hut is the made-up self, so there's no "you" really,
and it's pretty clear that neither you nor Shitou is
undying. He's been gone for over a millenium, and the
"you" that read the last sentence is gone, already just
an idea, a memory.

Identity and time are concepts; they are not truths.
We're engaged in words whose purpose is to show that
they are concepts, to show their limitations, to allow
consciousness to glimpse something beyond those limitations. The concept of an undying person is prob-
lematic; this does not refer to an immortal person.
Undying is shorthand for something indescribable; it's
not different from unborn. As Buddha said, everything
that comes to be must pass away. That which is undying never came into existence. In Zen there are many
references to "your face before you were born," which
points in the same direction as "the undying person in
the hut." We're talking about something not bound by
concepts of time or existence. Limitlessly free.

This undying person is you and is not you—or maybe
we could say the undying person isn't you and isn't not

you. No matter how we phrase it, it won't be quite true. Shitou is undying, he's long gone, and he's right here! You are invited to know him, to know me, to know yourself, to know each and all far beyond any knowing, to enter an intimacy that is not bound by time or any separation, but which destroys and excludes nothing. There is someone, unborn, in the midst of what you believe to be yourself. Who is this person?

# 32

## Here and Now

DON'T SEPARATE FROM THIS SKIN BAG
HERE AND NOW.

To practice the Buddha way is simple. Just come home to the present moment, to the here and now.

Even in the earliest days of Buddhism there were already thousands of teachings, but Buddha instructed that there is one practice that can open up the freedom and wisdom offered by all of them: mindfulness of the body through mindfulness of breath. To be mindful of breath is beautiful and powerful in and of itself, but it is also a technique that allows the mind to rest in the present, in this place, in the body, to truly taste the essential movement of our body that allows us to be, to see how what we think of as "outside" comes into us and sustains us, and how we give it right back without any planning or reviewing required. In this very moment air that has been all across the universe is in the process of becoming an essential part of your existence, and air is leaving your body that is an inseparable part of everything. Shitou's final instruction to realize timeless intimacy and arrive at the deep peace he shows throughout this poem is for us to just realize this body, in this place, at this time.

A couple of my friends love Shitou's use of the term "skin bag" here in this last line. It's a little laugh to remind us not to take ourselves too seriously, but sometimes people find it a little harsh and jarring. After all the beauty and ease of the earlier lines, the poem takes on a rough edge here at the end. This is actually a very old and powerful lesson; the idea of seeing the body as a skin bag goes back to the earliest Buddhist teachings. In the Four Foundations of Mindfulness Sutra, just after we learn mindfulness of breath, we're taught to be aware of the body as a bag of skin holding lots of nasty stuff. Yuck! This unpleasant image is here to remind us that being immersed in the present-moment sensations has the potential to just make us more attached to pleasurable sensations and averse to the ones we don't like. It is here to remind us of the impermanence of this body and all the sensations that go with it. It is here to remind us that if our practice is about getting something for ourselves it's just a part of the same process of attachment and aversion that causes all of our suffering. In this last line Shitou shows a middle way between deepening our connection to the present moment and letting go of what's here.

We need this line to remind us that when we are

comfortable it's good to stay in the moment without holding on to the feeling, and when we are uncomfortable (which is plenty of the time) we should not separate from the body. Moments of discomfort are precisely when the mind will want to take us away—into some idea of how things should be, how we can make them the way we want, or why things are all wrong. We find peace not by going away from our suffering but by completely offering ourselves to what is. There is no way to actually put this into words, as words inherently create ideas of things, which are separate, but we can truly not separate from this body here and now; already here, now, body and awareness are not separate things.

This truth can be realized through Buddhist practice. It may take many years of meditation, and we may find all kinds of frustration on the way, but it can be realized. It is in fact realizing itself right now; you can't avoid it.

So many times I've chanted this poem, seated and still after meditation, and this line helped me home. We chant this before lunch at Minnesota Zen Center on retreats, and I've chanted it many times along the lapping waters of Lake Calhoun and in the cold, breath-misting mornings in the Montana mountains. The natural imagery, the old man in a little hut on a mountainside, the shining window below the green pines, the wavelike reiteration of the themes of ease and calm, the flow from immediate and small inside the hut to the vast and inconceivable—the whole world included in that tiny home—they all come together and arrive in the heart. They hold forth a grand possibility of seeing how our small, immediate, moment-to-moment human effort is connected to the incredible vastness of everything, of everyone. Here at the end of this work we are encouraged to see that the way to realize this possibility, of making real the promise of having our lives be just a contribution to the wellness of all things, is simply to bring our whole selves to this body, this place, and this moment.

Here and now.

# Acknowledgments

I feel enormous gratitude for the many people who have helped me write this book.

I especially want to thank my family: Mom and dear departed Dad, my brother Chris, my boys Rocky and Max, and Lisa Wagner, all of whom have been extremely supportive and encouraging. Thanks to my dear Colleen, Daisy, Finn, and Delaney for bring lots of new love and inspiration over the last few years. The words in this book are essentially the fruit of the time I have been fortunate to spend doing Zen practice with my teacher Tim Burkett and my dear friends at Minnesota Zen Meditation Center, too many to name here, but especially: Rosemary Taylor, Wanda Isle, Ted O'Toole, Susan Nelson, Lee Lewis, Guy Gibbon, Stacy Lee King, and Kimberly Johnson. Andrea Martin and Philip Fuller provided invaluable input on my first attempts at the text for this book. Martin Lahn has been an incomparable friend and support to me and this work for, essentially, all time. Sharon Salzberg, Norman Fischer, Joan Halifax, Beata Grant, Jane Hirshfield, Red Pine, Mark Nunberg, Mark Berkson, and Scott Edelstein have all been very kind in taking time to support me as a new author and teacher. Taigen Dan Leighton has been very generous with his help as well as being an ongoing inspiration; without his vision in translating and publishing "Song of the Grass-Roof Hermitage" in his wonderful book *Cultivating the Empty Field* you certainly would not be reading this. Laura Cunningham, this book's editor, took a chance on me as a new author and has provided lots of encouragement, guidance, and great improvements to this book. Many thanks to my ashtanga yoga teacher, Lynn Thomasberg, and everyone at One Yoga, and to Christine and David on the homefront. Much gratitude to Bill W. and all his friends. Thank you to the trail crew in Glacier National Park and to everyone who pays taxes in the US so we can have these beautiful parks.

I have never met most of those without whom this work would not have been possible and there are many others I have forgotten, but in my heart I know they have brought me this opportunity. My deepest gratitude to all who do the practice of compassionate action and meditation, who sustain a tradition of kindness and peace of which I hope this book can be a part. A deep bow to you all, to everything.

# Selected Bibliography

Bhikku Bodhi. *In the Buddha's Words: An Anthology of Verses from the Pali Canon*. Boston: Wisdom Publications, 2005.

Cook, Francis. *Hua-Yen Buddhism: The Jewel Net of Indra*. New York: The Institute for Advanced Studies of World Religions, 1977.

Dumoulin, Heinrich. *Zen Buddhism: A History*. Bloomington, IN: World Wisdom, 2005

Easwaran, Eknath. *The Dhammapada*. Berkeley, CA: Nilgiri, 1985.

Foster, Nelson, and Jack Shoemaker. *The Roaring Stream: A New Zen Reader*. Hopewell, NJ: ECCO, 1996.

Grant, Beata. *Daughters of Emptiness: Poems of Chinese Buddhist Nuns*. Boston: Wisdom Publications, 2003.

Hixon, Lex. *Mother of the Buddhas: Meditations on the Prajnaparamita Sutra*. Wheaton, IL: Quest Books, 1993.

Kornfield, Jack. *The Wise Heart: A Guide to the Universal Teachings of Buddhist Psychology*. New York: Bantam Books, 2009.

Leighton, Taigen Dan. *Cultivating the Empty Field: The Silent Illumination of Zen Master Hongzhi*. San Francisco: North Point Press, 1991.

Lusthaus, Dan. *Buddhist Phenomenology: A Philosophical*

*Investigation of Yogacara Buddhism and the Ch'eng Wei-shih lun*. New York: RoutledgeCourzon, 2003.

Okumura, Shohaku. *Realizing Genjokoan: The Key to Dogen's Shobogenzo*. Boston: Wisdom Publications, 2010.

Schireson, Grace. *Zen Women: Beyond Tea Ladies, Iron Maidens, and Macho Masters*. Boston: Wisdom Publications, 2009.

Suzuki, Shunryu. *Branching Streams Flow in the Darkness: Zen Talks on the Sandokai*. Berkeley, CA: University of California Press, 2001.

Tanahashi, Kazuaki. *Moon in a Dewdrop: Writings of Zen Master Dogen*. New York: North Point Press, 1985

# Index

*Page numbers followed by "q" indicate quotations.*

austerity, 20, 23–24
enjoyment vs., 29–30
autonomy and interdependence, 65–66
awakening:
arising of liberation, 13
of Buddha, 87
readiness for, 77–78
See also enlightenment
awareness: of dependence, 142
See also consciousness

B
backing off practice, 153–54
backpacking trips, 18, 97, 106, 108
beginners: teaching, 48
being available, 36, 56–57, 132, 167
See also being present; generosity; kindness; offering of ourselves; service
being present, 28–30, 56–57, 80, 139, 165–66, 171–72
with the weeds, 32, 33, 35–38
belief in any god, 144
"Bind grasses to build a hut…," 151–54
Bodhidharma, 169–70q
bodhisattva, Great Vehicle, 73–74, 103
the body:
mindfulness of, 181–82

not separating from, 182–84
skin bag image, 182
breath: mindfulness of the body through mindfulness of, 181–82
breathing: noticing, 122
Buddha:
the All, 125
awakening, 87
enlightenment, 87–88, 89
first teaching, 138
on the house builder, 178
on love, 59–60
the Middle Way of, 23–24.
See also the Middle Way
as the original master, 87–89
renunciation of worldly life, 53
on right speech, 80
on the source, 143
on the teachings, 171, 173
on types of horses/people, 77–78
"What is Buddha?," 110–11
Buddha Way. See the Way
Buddhadharma: Shitou on, x–xi
See also the Way
Buddhism: Hua Yen, 65–66
See also early Buddhism; Yogacara; Zen
Buddhist monks, earliest: lifestyle, 18–19

building material options,
16–18
Burkett, Tim, 15q, 62q, 121q
on following the precepts,
50–51
on retreats, 56
Suzuki Roshi dreams, 83
Suzuki Roshi story, 66
Bush, George W.: just listening
to, 121

C
calm abiding, 40
"...can't compare with it,"
109–13
carrying around too much
time, 155
certainty: enmity between
reality and, 120–21
cessation of suffering, 36
change (transience), 84
steady practice amid, 98
*See also* impermanence
chanting or reciting texts, 7–8
the "Song of the Grass-Roof
Hermitage," 8–9, 177,
183–84
China, Shitou's, 53, 54
choice and karma, 158
choice vs. habit/unconscious
expression, 67–68
choosing to alleviate suffering,
159

choosing to live here, 125–26
Cold Mountain's works, 3–4
coming back/home to what is,
121, 137, 139, 155
commitment groups, 152–53
community practice, 49–50,
54
comparing: letting go, 111–13
compassion:
emptiness as, 44
with fear, 157
unconscious expression and,
67–68
concentrating practice,
69–72
concentration, right, 32, 33
concepts: words as, 179
connection (sense of), 143,
144
practice and, 142
consciousness, 46
awareness of dependence,
142
transforming of, 44
Consciousness-Only Bud-
dhism. *See* Yogacara
control: letting go, 33, 51, 107
cup holding experiment,
67–68

D
daily life. *See* life in the world
dangers of lofty language, 101

effort:
    right effort, 31–33
    self-centered, 131–32
Eightfold Path: inside and out-
        side of, 48
    See also right...
emptiness, 46
    as compassion, 44
    of fixed views, 46–47, 91–95
    Nagarjuna on, 94
    of self (ontological transpar-
        ency), 94, 103
encountering nature:
    hiking and backpacking trips,
        18, 106, 108
    and life in the world, 105–8
    meeting mountains, 107–8
encouragement:
    lofty language, 100–1, 102–4
    re meditation, 5, 99–100,
        112–13, 126–29, 151–54
    reading, 172
    Zen poems, 147
engaging life, 13–16, 138
    See also life in the world
engaging the Way: Dogen on,
        78
enjoyment, 26–30
    and attachment, 27–28
    vs. austerity, 29–30
    delight, 103
    mindfulness practice and,
        28–30

of the present moment, 28–30
enlightenment:
    of Buddha, 87–88, 89
    and death, 84
    Dogen on, 83–84
    the mind of, 35–38
    realizing the Way, 68, 183
    See also awakening; freedom;
        seeing things-as-they-are
enmity between certainty and
    reality, 120–21
ethics: teaching, 48, 50–51
everyday life. See life in the
    world

F
facing impermanence, 13–16
facing suffering, 13–14, 16,
    35–36, 165
family, author and, 18, 29, 97,
    106, 161–62
    See also father...; son...
family style of Zen, 145–49
father, author and, 83, 84–85
fear:
    and aggression, 164–65
    confusing with reality, 75
    experiencing and observing,
        74–75
    feelings with, 156–58
    function, 156
    karma and, 156–58
    of not-knowing, 120–21, 122

# About the Author

 Ben Connelly is a Soto Zen priest in the Katagiri lineage training with Tim Burkett at the Minnesota Zen Meditation Center. Connelly began teaching at MZMC in 2006, was ordained in 2009, and was made shuso, or head monk, in 2012. Ben is also a professional musician and developed and leads Mindfulness in the Mountains backpacking/meditation retreats in Northwest Montana.

# About Wisdom

Wisdom Publications is the leading publisher of contemporary and classic Buddhist books and practical works on mindfulness. Publishing books from all major Buddhist traditions, Wisdom is a nonprofit charitable organization dedicated to cultivating Buddhist voices the world over, advancing critical scholarship, and preserving and sharing Buddhist literary culture.

To learn more about us or to explore our other books, please visit our website at www.wisdompubs.org. You can subscribe to our eNewsletter, request a print catalog, and find out how you can help support Wisdom's mission either online or by writing to:

Wisdom Publications
199 Elm Street
Somerville, Massachusetts 02144 USA

You can also contact us at 617-776-7416 or info@wisdompubs.org.

Wisdom is a nonprofit, charitable 501(c)(3) organization, and donations in support of our mission are tax deductible.

Wisdom Publications is affiliated with the Foundation for the Preservation of the Mahayana Tradition (FPMT).

# Also Available from Wisdom Publications

## The Book of Mu
*Essential Writings of Zen's Most Important Koan*
James Ishmael Ford
Melissa Myozen Blacker
Foreword by John Tarrant
352 pages, $17.95

"The most important of all koans finally gets the attention it deserves. For those considering koan study, or just curious about this unique spiritual practice, this is a very valuable book."—David R. Loy, author of *Money, Sex, War, Karma*


## Together Under One Roof
*Making a Home of the Buddha's Household*
Lin Jensen
288 pages, $16.95

"This book will make you glad to have read it and glad to be alive."—Robert Langan, author of *Minding What Matters*

*Realizing Genjokoan*
*The Key to Dōgen's Shobogenzo*
Shohaku Okumura
Foreword by Taigen Dan Leighton
328 pages, $16.95

"A stunning commentary. Like all masterful commentaries, this one finds in the few short lines of the text the entire span of the Buddhist teachings."—*Buddhadharma: The Buddhist Review*

*Walking the Way*
*81 Zen Encounters with the Tao Te Ching*
Robert Rosenbaum
Foreword by Sojun Mel Weitsman
384 pages, $17.95

"An oasis of truth, compassion, laughter, and beauty. Welcome!"—Michael F. Hoyt, author of *Brief Psychotherapies*